Pluralism and the r

Pluralism and the religions

The theological and political dimensions

Edited by John D'Arcy May

CASSELL

Cassell
Wellington House, 125 Strand, London WC2R 0BB
PO Box 605, Herndon, VA 20172

Chapter 1 first appeared in *Ecumenical Review* (1997) and is published here with permission.

First published 1998

British Library Cataloguing-in-Publication Data
A catalogue record for this book is available from the British Library.

ISBN 0-304-70258-7
0-304-70259-5 (paperback)

Typeset by York House Typographic Ltd, London
Printed and bound in Great Britain by Biddles Ltd,
Guildford and King's Lynn.

Contents

Contributors

S. Wesley Ariarajah is an ordained Methodist minister from Sri Lanka. Formerly Director of the Sub-unit on Dialogue with People of Living Faiths at the World Council of Churches (WCC) in Geneva, and then Deputy General Secretary of the WCC, he is now Professor of Ecumenical Theology at Drew University, Madison, NJ. Among his publications are *The Bible and People of Other Faiths* (Geneva: WCC, 1985), *Hindus and Christians: A Century of Protestant Ecumenical Thought* (Amsterdam: Editions Rodopi, and Grand Rapids: Eerdmans, 1991) and *Did I Betray the Gospel? The Letters of Paul and the Place of Women* (Geneva: WCC, 1996).

Gavin D'Costa is Senior Lecturer in the Department of Theology and Religious Studies, University of Bristol. He was born in East Africa, from a Roman Catholic Goan background. He studied in England and has written *Theology and Religious Pluralism* (Oxford: Blackwell, 1986) and *John Hick's Theology of Religions* (Lanham, MD: University Press of America, 1987); and has edited *Resurrection Reconsidered* (Oxford: One World, 1995) and *Christian Uniqueness Reconsidered* (Maryknoll, NY: Orbis Books, 1990). He is currently writing a book on the Trinity and other religions. He is advisor to the Pontifical Commission for Inter-religious Dialogue, Vatican City, to the Roman Catholic Committee for Other Faiths in England and Wales, and to the Church of England Board of Mission.

Pia Gyger studied remedial education and psychology in Zürich. In 1976 she founded a therapeutic centre for young people, at the request of the Swiss Federal Department of Justice. In 1982 she was elected Director General of the St. Katherina-Werk, a lay Catholic community for women in Basle, which she opened up for men and couples from different Christian denominations. After ten years' Zen training with Hugo Enomiya-Lassalle SJ she had her first sojourn with Yamada Roshi in Japan in 1984, completing her *koan*-work after his death with Aitken Roshi in Hawaii, from whom she received teaching permission in 1990. In 1997 she was made an Independent Master of Zen. Meanwhile, in 1986 she founded the Project for the Encounter of World Religions and in 1992 the Project for the Development of a Spiritual-Political Consciousness. She also founded a school in a slum in Manila in 1989. In 1994 she handed over responsibility for the St. Katherina-Werk community, and in 1996 she co-founded with Fr Niklaus Brantschen SJ the Institute for Spirituality in Politics and the Economy at the Lassalle-Haus in Bad Schönbrunn near Zug, Switzerland.

Ursula King STL (Paris), MA (Delhi), PhD (London), Hon. DD (Edinburgh), FRSA is Professor in the Department of Theology and Religious Studies, University of Bristol, England. She is a former President of the European Society of Women in Theological Research (1993–95) and of the British Association for the Study of Religions (1991–94). She has published numerous articles and books, among others *Women and Spirituality: Voices of Protest and Promise* (London: Macmillan, and University Park: Penn State Press, 1993) and edited several volumes: *Turning Points in Religious Studies* (Edinburgh: T. & T. Clark, 1990); *Feminist Theology from the Third World: A Reader* (London: SPCK, and Maryknoll, NY: Orbis Books, 1994); and *Religion and Gender* (Oxford: Basil Blackwell, 1995). She is also one of the co-editors of *Religion in Europe: Contemporary Perspectives* (Kampen: Kok Pharos, 1994). In earlier years she published a German translation of the Trinitarian treatises of Marius Victorinus and two studies on Pierre Teilhard de Chardin. She has written a new biography of Teilhard de Chardin, *Spirit of Fire: The Life and Vision of Pierre Teilhard de Chardin* (Maryknoll, NY: Orbis Books, 1996). In spring 1996 she gave the Bampton Lectures at Oxford University which are published as *Christ in All Things: Exploring Spirituality with Teilhard de Chardin* (London: SCM, and Maryknoll, NY: Orbis Books, 1997). Most recently, she has edited *Faith and Praxis in a Postmodern Age* (London: Cassell, 1998).

Paul F. Knitter is Professor of Theology at Xavier University, Cincinnati. Before moving to Xavier University in 1975, he was a member of the Society of the Divine Word and taught at Catholic Theological Union in Chicago. He received a Licentiate in Theology from the Pontifical Gregorian University in Rome (1966) and a doctorate from the University of Marburg (1972). Over the past years most of his research and publications have dealt with religious pluralism and interreligious dialogue. He is General Editor of Orbis Books' series 'Faith Meets Faith' and is the author of *No Other Name? A Critical Survey* *of Christian Attitudes Toward World Religions* (Maryknoll, NY: Orbis Books, and London: SCM, 1985) and editor with John Hick of *The Myth of Christian Uniqueness: Toward a Pluralistic Theology of Religions* (Maryknoll, NY: Orbis Books, 1987; London: SCM, 1988). He has just finished two books exploring the relationship between interreligious dialogue and global responsibility: *One Earth, Many Religions* (Maryknoll, NY: Orbis Books, 1995) and *Jesus and the Other Names* (Maryknoll, NY: Orbis Books, 1996). Over the past ten years, Knitter has also been active in various peace groups working with the churches of El Salvador. He is presently a member of the Board of Directors of CRISPAZ (Christians for Peace in El Salvador).

John D'Arcy May was born in Melbourne, Australia. After receiving a Dr. theol. in Ecumenics from the University of Münster in 1975 he was *wissenschaftlicher Assistent* at the Catholic Ecumenical Institute there, 1975–82, receiving a Dr. phil. in History of Religions from the University of Frankfurt in 1983. He was Ecumenical Research Officer with the Melanesian Council of Churches, Port Moresby, and Research Associate at the Melanesian Institute, Goroka, Papua New Guinea, 1983–87, and Director of the Irish School of Ecumenics in Dublin, 1987–90, where he is now Associate Professor of Interfaith Dialogue and Ethics. He has been a visiting professor in Fribourg, Switzerland (1982), Frankfurt am Main (1988) and Wollongong, Australia (1994). His publications include *Sprache der Ökumene – Sprache der Einheit. Die Einheit der Menschheit: Zukünftige Grundlage der theologischen Ethik der Katholischen Kirche und des Ökumenischen Rats der Kirchen?* (Bonn: Linguistica Biblica, 1976); *Meaning, Consensus and Dialogue in Buddhist–Christian Communication: A Study in the Construction of Meaning* (Berne: Peter Lang, 1984); and *Christus Initiator: Theologie im Pazifik* (Düsseldorf: Patmos, 1990). He has edited *Living Theology in Melanesia: A Reader* (Goroka: The Melanesian Institute, 1985).

J. Rosario Narchison obtained Master's degrees in both Philosophy and Theology at the Jnana Deepa Vidvapeeth (Institute of Philosophy and Religion) at Pune, India, and a doctorate in Historical Theology from the Lutheran School of Theology, Chicago, USA. He worked for ten years as the pastor of a Roman Catholic parish in South India, and for six years as the Dean of the Indian School of Ecumenical Theology, Bangalore, India. His publications include articles on fundamentalism, secularism and communalism in such Indian reviews as *Journal of Dharma* and *Vidyajyoti*. Currently he is the editor of the *Indian Church History Review*. His latest publication is *YMCA as an Ecumenical Movement* (Bangalore: YMCA Training Centre, 1995).

Introduction: the theory and practice of pluralism

John D'Arcy May

Theological debate about the dialogue of religions has tended to take as its point of reference understandings of pluralism which originated in the European Enlightenment. It is beginning to dawn on Western theologians that there may be alternative models of pluralism with roots in other cultures and religions. Must we reckon not only with varieties of religion, but also with those of pluralism? Is the liberal tradition of tolerance an adequate framework for theological responses to the problems raised by feminists and ecologists? Does the invocation of 'pluralism' still make sense as a theological prescription for dealing with the religious repercussions of postmodernism and globalization? Must we now get used to asking 'Whose pluralism?' as well as 'Which religion?'

Arising out of our concerns in the fields of ecumenism and peace studies, these questions prompted us at the Irish School of Ecumenics to call together a group of scholars who could provide some new perspectives. In Dublin from 25 to 27 November 1995, 130 participants from Ireland and other parts of Europe gathered to discuss the relationship between pluralism and the religions in workshops on dialogue and revelation, ecology and religious education, scripture and ecumenical practice, Judaism, Islam and Buddhist meditation. These took place in the framework of lectures by two keynote speakers from Asia, Wesley Ariarajah from Sri Lanka and Rosario Narchison from India, complemented by two theologians of dialogue, Gavin D'Costa of Bristol and Paul Knitter of Cincinnati, who took the discussion to the cutting edge of contemporary theological endeavour, and two women practitioners of dialogue, Ursula King of Bristol and Pia Gyger of Basle, who pointed to new developments in the theory and practice of dialogue demanded by the claims of women and the poor to be active participants in a truly global dialogue of solidarity.

The theological dimension

Both Wesley Ariarajah and Ursula King emphasize the failure of Christian ecumenical theology, in the one case to make sense of plurality and in the other to integrate the feminine in its response to religious pluralism. The practice of interreligious dialogue, according to Ariarajah, has revolutionized the Christian concept of mission and contributes powerfully to overcoming Christian divisions. But the pluralism of religions is still not recognized as the foremost new challenge facing Christian theology. Gavin D'Costa contrasts a highly original 're-reading' of a familiar text from Genesis (18:1–15) in the light of Rublev's icon of the Trinity with a theological interpretation of Jyoti Sahi's painting *The Word Made Flesh*. By 'negotiating' the meanings of both Jewish and Christian scriptures with Russian Orthodox tradition and Indian folk culture, D'Costa demonstrates how the dialogue of religions can take place at the very heart of Christian theology. Questions such as the imperializing tendency of this theology and its tolerance of syncretism are thereby posed in entirely new ways.

Ursula King, anticipating comments by both Narchison and Gyger, sees both the feminist and the interfaith movements as children of a democratic, secular, post-colonial society and identifies the challenges they pose to one another: if the dialogue of religions is still an exclusively male affair, feminist theology by and large remains oblivious of its implications. The global dialogue of women which is in fact taking place subverts interreligious dialogue by introducing a hitherto unsuspected dimension of Otherness, while the political dimension of interreligious dialogue is still not appreciated by feminists.

The political dimension

For Rosario Narchison, speaking from the perspective of theological education for the Indian context at the Indian School of Ecumenical Theology (ISET) in Bangalore, ecumenism means pluralism, and education for pluralism is education for secularism. India, with a plural society in a monolithic state, has to find its own forms of both pluralism and democracy, breaking the Western mould imposed on it in colonial times with its legacy of religio-political 'communalism'. Imported Western theologies are inappropriate in such a situation, in which it must be possible to develop a Hindu theological perspective if theology is to be truly ecumenical. The founder of ISET, M. A. Thomas, went so far as to say: 'Outside the world there is no salvation!'

This parallels precisely Edward Schillebeeckx's adaptation of an ancient Christian adage as cited by Paul Knitter: *extra mundum nulla salus*. In the postmodern context the very possibility of the 'global ethic' now being proposed by some theologians of dialogue must first be established. Knitter insists that every religious tradition has both prophetical and mystical strands which are not opposite but complementary. The 'universe story', which enhances ecological awareness but depends for its telling on Western science, must be complemented by the common ethical story of humankind. This can happen if solidarity with the suffering is perceived to underlie cultural and religious diversity, thereby making possible the participation of the suffering in the dialogue itself.

Like King, Knitter notes the patriarchal bias of interreligious dialogue, and he shares with Pia Gyger a concern for the survival of all life as the new and theologically decisive motivation for dialogue. Both King and Gyger refer to the prophetic vision of Teilhard de Chardin when they emphasize the scope of the evolutionary cultural and political developments we must now anticipate. For Gyger, these will involve planetary structures for a pan-federal, democratic world community which will include a worldwide partnership of men and women. Speaking from her experience in helping to establish the Institute for Spirituality in Politics and the Economy near Zug in Switzerland, she highlights the neglect of world poverty and the growth of expenditure on armaments as indices of the transformation of attitudes which co-operation between religions must accomplish. As we face this task, she says, plurality is both treasure and tribulation.

This last remark has a particular resonance in Ireland, and a special significance attaches to the fact that these papers were first presented to a largely Irish audience to commemorate the twenty-fifth anniversary of the Irish School of Ecumenics. Pluralism has become a key issue in the long search for a peaceful solution of the 'Irish problem'. It was regularly mentioned by President Mary Robinson in her major speeches, and it is seen by leaders on both sides of the border as either an opportunity or a threat, as the case may be. Both the Republic of Ireland and Northern Ireland are more religiously plural than has hitherto been noticed, and each in its characteristically different way is becoming culturally, religiously and politically more pluralist. These twin developments rewrite the equation of a conflict that is undeniably, if not entirely, 'religious'.

In presenting these innovative papers to a wider public, I should like to thank my colleagues at the Irish School of Ecumenics who bore with me while the conference was in preparation, those who led workshops and participated in the lively and controversial discussions which ensued, the principal speakers for preparing their manuscripts for publication, my students who helped with the index, and Gillian Paterson and her colleagues whose professionalism turned them into a book.

Dublin, Easter 1997

Part One

Pluralism and dialogue: the theological dimension

1

The impact of interreligious dialogue on the ecumenical movement[1]

S. Wesley Ariarajah

Has the Ecumenical Movement a Future? is the provocative title of a book published in 1974. The author was Willem Visser 't Hooft, the first general secretary of the World Council of Churches (WCC). In this book, first given as a series of lectures in May 1972 in the Netherlands, Visser 't Hooft traces what he considers to be the four distinct periods of ecumenical history, and the three fundamental questions that face the ecumenical movement. For our purposes here, I should like to recall the three 'central questions' that he thought 'dominated the present ecumenical agenda':

> – Is the ecumenical movement suffering from institutional paralysis?
> – Should we replace mission as it has been practised up till now by a dialogue with the other religions?
> – Should the ecumenical movement follow the agenda of the Church – or the agenda of the world?[2]

It is of course tempting, whether one agrees with Visser 't Hooft's conclusions or not, to dwell on the analysis he makes of these vital questions from his long, sustained and deep involvement in the ecumenical movement. But what is interesting is that Visser 't Hooft, who was deeply motivated by the search for the visible unity of the church and the church's mission in the world, and whose basic theological formation remained Barthian to the very end, should admit in 1972 that one of the most important questions that faces the future of the ecumenical movement is the issue of 'dialogue and mission'. Only a decade earlier Visser 't Hooft would have insisted that the missionary mandate and what it called for was so self-evident that the question did not deserve even a discussion.

But as one who always had his fingers on the pulse of the ecumenical movement, he was able to discern the increasing impact of interreligious dialogue, and the difficult and often painful and deeply divisive issues it raised for the Christian understanding of mission, especially in relation to people who live by other religious traditions.

But before entering this discussion, it is appropriate to say a word about the term 'ecumenical'. When used in the Christian context, it denotes all the movements that contribute to the search for the unity of the church and of humankind. Therefore, there are many partners within the one ecumenical movement, and the emergence of inter-religious dialogue has had different degrees of impact on them. During and after the Second Vatican Council, for instance, the Roman Catholic Church has developed teachings and engaged in activities that have made a significant difference to the Christian response to the inter-religious reality.

For the purposes of this presentation, however, I hope to stay with the impact that interreligious dialogue has had on one of the instruments and expressions of the ecumenical movement, namely the WCC. Even though it will, of necessity, be only a partial look, I hope that the other presentations will help us to develop and appreciate the larger picture.

It is also important to say a word about the terms 'interreligious' and 'interfaith'. Wilfred Cantwell Smith, perhaps the most creative and courageous of the pioneers in the field, and a mentor to so many of us, insists rightly that we should define our terms to avoid confusion. He himself has made helpful distinctions between the terms 'religion', 'belief', 'faith', etc. But, alas, in the explosion of the literature in this field, 'interreligious' and 'interfaith' are used interchangeably, almost beyond recovery! This will be evident in my use of these terms as well.

Dialogue and the missionary mandate

Visser 't Hooft's concern about the impact of interfaith dialogue on the missionary enterprise was only natural, because one of the earliest imperatives for the modern ecumenical movement itself came from the sense of urgency in relation to world mission. It was the conviction that the 'decisive hour of Christian mission' had come that impelled John R. Mott to call the World Mission Conference of 1910, with the primary purpose of pooling resources and developing a common strategy for the 'world's conquest' for Christ. The task of 'taking the Gospel to all the regions of the world' was seen to be of such paramount importance that one had to transcend and eventually overcome the theological and confessional differences among Christians that hampered its progress.

Therefore, it is important to recognize that even though the missionary movement joined the WCC only at the third assembly in New

Delhi in 1961, it was the first of the movements to constitute itself as an ecumenical force, laying the firm foundations for the International Missionary Council already in 1910. And the missionary movement decided to stay out, when the Faith and Order and Life and Work movements came together in 1948 to form the WCC, so that its focused attention on world mission would not be watered down by being part of a wider movement. Such were the deep convictions on mission that motivated the early ecumenical endeavours.

No doubt there were voices from the beginning that called for a different approach to other religious traditions. But they were marginal within the movement and had little or no impact on the primary thrust of 'winning the world for Christ'. Even though leading missiologists of the movement, like Hendrik Kraemer, had close contact with people of other faiths, the issues of mission and the theology of religions were matters for internal discussion within the church and the missionary movement. The peoples of other faiths were the objects of the missionary outreach.

The first breakthrough came when in 1956 the study centres around the world were asked to pick up a study project, 'Word of God and the living faiths of men' (*sic*), to continue the inconclusive and deeply divisive debate of Tambaram (1938) over Hendrik Kraemer's preparatory volume, *The Christian Message in a Non-Christian World*. In carrying out the project, P. D. Devanandan, Director of the Study Centre (Christian Institute for the Study of Religion and Society – CISRS) in Bangalore, who was primarily interested in 'nation-building' in postcolonial India, decided that a Christian discussion of the living faiths must be informed by real encounters with persons of other faith traditions.

This was an important landmark in the history of the movement, because it established the principle that the peoples of other faiths should no longer be the objects of our discussions, but partners in our conversation. The concept of 'dialogue' was born, and it was to make a decisive impact on all subsequent discussions on mission within the ecumenical movement.

The confidence created by the actual encounters with people of other faiths led to the plea for what Stanley Samartha called 'a post-Kraemer theology of mission' that would no longer see people of other faiths as 'non-Christian', but as people who live by other faith convictions. The passion with which this new view was held is reflected in an article that Samartha wrote for the *Indian Journal of Theology*. Ian D. L. Clark, who surveyed this period, calls the following passage Samartha's incidental 'final epitaph on Kraemer':

With the passing away of Kraemer an era in the history of the theology
of mission has ended. It was an era which, at its height, was marked by
aggressive certainty, unbound enthusiasm, a sureness of direction and
assured hope for the coming harvest. There is no doubt that Kraemer
dominated the scene and, with his massive scholarship and real
concern for the mission of the church, upheld many drooping spirits in
Mission Boards. But times have changed. The clear-cut division of the
world into Christian and non-Christian made in his Tambaram book is
no longer valid. Today one talks about Christian faith and other faiths.[3]

It is not my intention to trace here the history of the subsequent
developments; but, as Samartha had said, times had in fact changed,
and the whole experience of the interfaith encounters was soon to be
expressed within the WCC in the creation of a new sub-unit for
'Dialogue with People of Living Faiths and Ideologies', and an exploration of the meaning of 'Seeking Community' with people of other
faiths.

The far-reaching, decisive and deeply disturbing impact that interreligious dialogue has had on the understanding of mission within the
ecumenical movement was witnessed to in the impassioned, acrimon-
ious and deeply divisive debate over interfaith dialogue at the Nairobi
Assembly (1975). It was the inevitable 'showdown' within the ecumenical fellowship, between the traditional understanding of mission as
converting others to become Christians and the emerging concept of
'mutual witness', where dialogue was seen not as yet another tool for
mission but as a context in which authentic witness might be given.

Every arsenal at the disposal of the traditional understanding of
mission was brought out to ward off the dangers presented by interreligious dialogue to mission and evangelism – syncretism, com-
promise of the uniqueness and finality of Christ, loss of mission and
spiritual confusion. If 1910 was the 'decisive hour of Christian mission'
for John R. Mott, Nairobi (1975) was 'the decisive hour for interfaith
dialogue' for Stanley Samartha. What saved the hour, however, was the
convincing witness given by those, mainly from Asia (like Lynn A. de
Silva, J. R. Chandran and others), who were actual practitioners of
dialogue. The assembly, though made up of a majority who were
inclined to affirm the traditional understanding of mission, was not
willing to deny or betray the experience of those who had entered into
a new relationship with their neighbours. In so doing, it also opened a
new door to the understanding of mission within the ecumenical
movement.[4]

The impact of interreligious dialogue on the understanding of mission was such that the *Guidelines on Dialogue*, drawn up within two
years of the Nairobi Assembly, primarily to deal with the fears and

suspicions vented there, was able to say that 'dialogue has a distinctive and rightful place within Christian life'. It went further to affirm that 'In giving their witness they (Christians) recognize that in most circumstances today the spirit of dialogue is necessary'.

And then, the clear affirmation:

> For this reason we do not see dialogue and the giving of witness as standing in any contradiction to one another. Indeed, as Christians enter dialogue with their commitment to Jesus Christ, time and again the relationship of dialogue gives opportunity for authentic witness. Thus to the member churches of the WCC we feel able with integrity to commend the way of dialogue as one in which Jesus Christ can be confessed in the world today; at the same time we feel able with integrity to assure our partners in dialogue that we come not as manipulators but as genuine fellow-pilgrims, to speak with them of what we believe God to have done in Jesus Christ who has gone before us, but whom we seek to meet anew in dialogue.[5]

I have recalled yet again this much-quoted passage from the *Guidelines on Dialogue* because in addition to what it says, it also symbolizes a significant moment in the ecumenical movement. If Samartha was convinced that an era of understanding on mission came to an end with Kraemer, this statement, in a real sense, marked the beginning of a new era in the understanding of mission. While there is still a plurality of understandings on the nature and practice of mission within the ecumenical fellowship, and there would be sections within it that would still gladly align themselves with Kraemer, no discussion on mission within the ecumenical movement today can ignore the reality and practice of interfaith relations.

In fact, the Vancouver Assembly chose the word 'witness' in preference to 'mission', and its section on 'Witness in a divided world' spoke about dialogue as an 'encounter where people holding different claims about ultimate reality can meet and explore these claims in a context of mutual respect'. It went even further to say that 'From dialogue we expect to discern more about how God is active in the world, and to appreciate for their own sake the insights and experiences people of other faiths have of ultimate reality'.[6]

This bold assertion of the presence of God in the experiences of others was again challenged, also by some of the same voices heard at Nairobi, but the report, which went much further than Nairobi, was generally acceptable to the assembly.

There is no need to labour the point. One can illustrate this development also from several other official statements, including those from the World Mission Conference in San Antonio or the Seventh Assembly in Canberra. The point is that the practice of interreligious dialogue has brought about a radical revolution within the simple, straightforward and clear-cut missionary mandate inherited by the ecumenical movement in its early years.

Some of those who led the missionary movement prior to this decisive impact of dialogue on our understanding of mission, of whom Bishop Lesslie Newbigin is a good example, refuse to accept that the revolution has taken place. Instead they blame dialogue for the considerable confusion within conservative circles on the purpose and goals of mission when religions, freed from the power distortions of the colonial era, are asserting themselves as equal partners.

But the profound crisis within the conservative missionary enterprise and the temptation to turn to fundamentalism can never be faced unless one concedes the impact the practice of interreligious dialogue has made on our understanding and practice of mission. It is an impact that has made a difference. It is not possible to return to Tambaram.

The search for a theological foundation

The second, and equally important, impact has been a theological one. As interfaith dialogue became a serious and more widespread activity, the movement became increasingly aware that the churches did not have a theology that could make sense of the challenge of plurality.

If one were to revisit the Nairobi debate and analyse the fears, anxieties and theological reservations that prompted the controversy over dialogue, one would soon realize that the underlying problem was that the churches did not have a theological handle to take on board what was being offered in the area of 'seeking community with people of other faiths'.

The Protestant churches within the WCC had interpretations of the person and work of Christ, concepts of revelation and salvation, theologies of mission and a theology of religions that in the final analysis reduced the world of other faiths into no more than a vast and endless mission field. The emphasis on the 'one' – one Lord, one faith, one saviour, one way, one community, etc. – which for effective missionary purposes was reinforced as also the 'only' made the Christians the least equipped to live in a religiously plural world. If the Orthodox theological tradition had better handles to deal with plurality, it was not evident, at least in the Nairobi debate, that it had been developed to deal with the challenge of religious plurality.

At Nairobi, therefore, many traditional theologians experienced the dialogue venture as something that shook the theological foundations of the church. It not only challenged traditional Christology and missiology, it also threatened to take away the very *raison d'être*, purpose, of the church *vis-à-vis*, face to face with, people of other faiths. As someone who participated in the Nairobi debate, I could not help feeling that there were many who, at the religious level, would not know what else to do with a Hindu than to convert him or her!

The 'missionary obligation', as traditionally interpreted, needed the world of other faiths as the 'mission field'; without it, not only the missionary enterprise but also faith itself was in danger. Many experienced the dialogue debate as a 'life-and-death question' not only for missions, but also for the church. In this respect it was a genuine debate struggling to come to terms with a decisive moment in the ecumenical journey.

In reality, however, it was a fresh theological challenge to the ecumenical movement. The movement did not have a theology of plurality. It did not know how to talk about Jesus Christ and witness to what God has done in him except in Christocentric and exclusivist terms. It could not make theological sense of other religious experiences and of those who had heard the gospel but had chosen not to become part of the church.

Those who have followed the development of the dialogue ministry of the WCC would know that in the periods following Nairobi and Vancouver, the then Sub-unit on Dialogue attempted to respond to this theological challenge posed by interfaith dialogue to the churches and the ecumenical movement. The study booklet on *My Neighbour's Faith and Mine – Theological Discoveries in Interfaith Dialogue* (in 16 languages), the Risk book on *The Bible and People of Other Faiths* (ten languages), both aimed at the congregations, and a series of theological consultations on the theology of religions, including Baar I and Baar II, are responses to the theological impact of interfaith dialogue on the WCC.[7]

This significant theological impact of interfaith dialogue on the movement is also attested by the several hundreds of volumes and the thousands of articles that have appeared over the past ten years, in all parts of the world, seeking to find an adequate theological basis for a new relationship among faith communities. It has been said that the contemporary Christian encounter with the people of other faiths, especially in the context of dialogue, has to be compared to the first encounters of the Jewish-Christian theology with Hellenistic thought and culture; a long process may be ahead, but nothing can be the same again.

The change of religious consciousness

What we have dealt with so far is the more obvious, direct and discernible impact that the interreligious reality has had on the ecumenical movement. But what is more important is the change of religious climate that the phenomenon of interreligious dialogue has brought about in the religious atmosphere, which is more difficult to pin down.

In recent years more and more people have become deeply concerned about the increase of fundamentalism within all religious traditions and the several conflicts around the world where religious symbolism and sentiments are used and abused for social and political ends. This is an important concern, and calls for careful analysis and concerted action, so that some of the advances made in interfaith relations are not lost to political expediency.

This is, however, only one aspect of the reality. The other is that we are witnessing today a remarkable lowering of the barriers that have separated religious traditions for centuries, resulting in what might be described as an emergence of an 'interfaith culture' in the religious scene.

The proliferation of local dialogues, the popularity of interfaith movements and organizations, the readiness to engage in interfaith worship, the increased instances of interfaith marriages, the use of each other's spiritual practices, the growth of popular interfaith literature, the greater willingness to engage together on common issues and the fact that every respectable Christian theologian today feels compelled to deal with the interfaith questions are only the symptoms of a much deeper reality. I hope it is not too much to assume that they are only the tip of the iceberg, and underneath it is a whole new religious consciousness in the making. If I wanted to single out the most challenging and demanding impact of the interfaith reality on the ecumenical movement it has to be this change of consciousness. As in many instances of social change, not everyone recognizes or discerns the changes that are taking place, even in their own consciousness.

One of the problems faced within the movement is that not everyone is agreed on whether this change is for the better or the worse, whether it is of the Spirit or not, whether God is calling us to walk in faith on an uncharted road or whether the urgency is to get back on to the known road.

Some have dismissed the whole reality as 'New Age thinking', seeing behind it all 'a neo-Hindu-Buddhist plot' for the 'spiritual takeover' of the West. Some others, like Lesslie Newbigin, while recognizing the need to be in good relations with peoples of other faiths, are alarmed by the theological challenge, and see the situation as a new danger to the ecumenical movement. In their view, we must dig our trenches even deeper in order to guard what they consider to be the 'truth of the gospel' against relativism. Newbigin argues that since Christians have been shown Jesus Christ as the one road to follow, what is needed today is to reaffirm the 'logic of mission' and regain our 'confidence in the gospel'.[8]

Visser 't Hooft, with whom we began this enquiry, while also affirming the need to respect other religions, was more concerned with the emergence in the contemporary world of 'a cult of life' or 'neo-paganism' that pervades also some parts of the interfaith movement. Defining 'paganism' as the glorification of life for its own sake without any reference to God, Visser 't Hooft declares that 'the religion of life and the faith in the living God are totally incompatible' with each other.[9]

While these reactions are to be expected and taken seriously, the reality is that the interfaith dialogue has shaken deeply the theological and religious consciousness of the ecumenical movement. If the 'oikoumene' is the whole inhabited earth, and if God is the creator of all that is and intends to bring all things to fulfilment, it is no longer conceivable that large sections of the life of the people can be left outside the focus of the ecumenical movement.

In interfaith dialogue we have learned that the conviction and confidence that a group has that it is called to give a specific witness to God and how God deals with humankind in itself does not separate it from the human family. More importantly, it does not provide the reason not to discern God's life with all peoples or to disregard peoples' experiences of their life with God. Wilfred Cantwell Smith, in his inimitable style, has complained that the problem about doing theology without any consciousness and knowledge of other religious traditions and of the faith of others is that one leaves out much of the data needed to do theology. Already 30 years ago, he predicted that the 'time will soon be with us' when a theologian who attempts to do theology without this consciousness will be 'as hopelessly out of date as one who attempts to construct an intellectual position unaware that Aristotle has taught, or unaware that the earth is a minor planet in a galaxy that is vast only by terrestrial standards'.[10]

What the interfaith dialogue has done to the ecumenical movement is to signal that 'this time' that Cantwell Smith has been speaking about has in fact come. We may still not be fully equipped to face this time but there are clear indications that the ecumenical movement has read the signals correctly. It is not surprising then, that the WCC could no longer plan its major assemblies, its Justice, Peace and Integrity of Creation (JPIC) Convocation (Seoul, 1990), or even its World Mission Conference (San Antonio, 1989), without at least a symbolic presence of persons of other faith traditions. And on such issues as the ecological crisis, human rights, peace, reconciliation, AIDS, etc., and on such concerns as justice for women and children, the questions that are often raised are: 'What do other religious traditions say about this?' or 'Which persons of other faiths can contribute to this discussion?' The other facet of this same development is that many such issues, which at one time were subjects of discussion within each of the religious communities, have now entered the widening agenda of the interfaith organizations.

If the time is indeed here, our response so far has been only symbolic. This is because of the lack of 'theological courage' on the part of many to take down some of the old pillars on which the movement was built, even though they can no longer support the structure. The people who are crying 'wolf!', accusing the ecumenical leadership of taking the movement down the path of destruction, simply pile up arguments based on the old presuppositions, not realizing that it is those very presuppositions and the whole theological tradition built on them that is being questioned and set aside.

What we have is new wine. Jesus taught that one should not put new wine into old wineskins because it will ruin both the wineskins and the wine. The new wine needs new wineskins.

One of the new wineskins in the making since the New Delhi Assembly has been the concept of 'humankind'. This came into prominence in order to take account of the universal dimension and scope of the gospel message. It is noteworthy that the Uppsala Assembly (1968), which was the first assembly to commend interfaith dialogue to the churches, reaffirmed the study on 'The unity of the church and the unity of mankind' (later changed to 'humankind'). What was significant about it was that the study was to be undertaken within the Faith and Order Commission that had traditionally concentrated primarily on doctrinal issues in Christian unity. Had the time come when the unity and renewal of 'humankind', the whole oikoumene, would become the focus of ecumenical concern?

One of the sections that dealt with this question at the Faith and Order plenary commission meeting in Leuven (Louvain), Belgium (1971) was on 'The unity of the church and the encounter with living faiths', showing the commission's sensitivity that humankind does live by other faith traditions as well. But a rereading of the report of the section discussion shows how the whole question was approached from a very narrow and exclusive perspective:

> Is the encounter with other faiths an encounter 'in Christ'? Does God reveal Himself outside the specific stream of Christian history? Must Christians believe other faiths contain authentic revelation before true dialogue can begin (sharp division here)? ... How can the particularity of Christian faith be claimed as the basis for mankind's unity amidst other religious and ideological claims of a similar kind?[11]

The quotation is illustrative of the Council's apparent inability to deal with any question except from a Christocentric, often even from a Christo-monistic, standpoint. In fact the whole of the WCC's concern for 'humankind', 'the whole human family', the 'wider oikoumene', etc. has for a long time been caught within what Konrad Raiser has called the paradigm of 'Christocentric universalism'.

In his book *Ecumenism in Transition*, Raiser says that what we are witnessing today is a paradigm shift in the ecumenical movement that seeks to take the 'oikos', the household of God, in its true and full meaning as locus of God's concern:

> The 'oikoumene' then is not a description of a given state of affairs. It is not a matter of structures, but of dynamic, real relationships ... When we say 'oikoumene', we are not referring to global abstractions, such as 'one world', the 'whole human race' or 'one united world church'. We are speaking of actual and at the same time endangered connections and relationships between churches, between cultures, between people and human societies in their infinite variety, and between the world of humankind and creation as a whole.

And he sees relationships as the very essence of life and of the oikoumene:

> All human beings in their living, knowing, and acting are from the very beginning related to their world, to other people, to their living environment, to those things that are necessary to life. Being-in-relationship is as much a part of our nature as being-in-oneself ... Human knowledge is accompanied by the quest for connections. But it does not create these connections, but rather perceives even more comprehensively the original interconnectedness, which was there even before we are aware of it.[12]

The contrast of the approach taken by the 'Unity of the church and unity of humankind' study in 1971 and that seen in Raiser's statement in many ways is indicative of the change in perception and orientation that has been and is taking place within the ecumenical movement. The impact of interreligious dialogue (among other factors) is one of the catalysts of this change.

It is interesting to note that while the first general secretary saw, in 1972, the impact of interfaith dialogue on mission as the second of the crucial issues facing the ecumenical movement, the present general secretary, reflecting on the same question 20 years later, places the challenge of religious pluralism to Christocentrism as the first of 'The new challenges facing the ecumenical movement' that is bringing about a paradigm shift.[13]

The new or wider ecumenism

Some within ecumenical circles are uncomfortable with the emergence of such phrases as 'new ecumenism', 'wider ecumenism', 'ecumenism of religions', etc., fearing that it signals the end of the 'Christian ecumenism' that was primarily concerned with the recovery of the visible unity of the church.

This is an unfounded fear, because there is nothing in interfaith encounters that calls a halt to the search for Christian unity. The experience of Christians who have been in dialogue with persons of other faiths is that the dialogue partner never treats you as a 'Reformed', 'Lutheran', 'Anglican' or 'Orthodox', but as a 'Christian'. It is quite fascinating to watch how Christians are forced, in actual dialogue situations, to look for common language to talk about the fundamentals of their faith. They are left with little choice but to overcome their differences momentarily, or to show them as different approaches to the commonly held beliefs that keep them in that faith community.

It is in interfaith encounters that I became convinced that Christians can in fact speak a common language about their faith if they really wanted to, or had to, and that it is possible to bear authentic witness to Christ without having to use exclusive language. It is in this sense that Kenneth Cracknell sees in the interfaith encounter a hope for the renewal of the church.

The call for a 'wider ecumenism' that is provoked, among other factors, by the impact of the several decades of interreligious relations is not a cry, as said above, against Christian ecumenism, but a call to recover the scope and the depth of what should really be encompassed in the term 'ecumenical'. It arises from the awareness that the whole world, all its peoples and all their histories are subjects of God's concern. It is based on the conviction that the unity that God intends is for all people, and not for some. It comes from the realization that God's creation, in its goodness and variety, as also in all its complexities, problems, sufferings, alienation and rebellion, is the locus of the activity of the Spirit of God. It affirms, as Raiser says, that all of life, rooted as it is in God, is interrelated from the beginning, and that what we are after is to perceive, enter into and rejoice in this 'original interconnectedness' which 'was there even before we became aware of it'.[14]

The call for 'a global ethic' at the Parliament of the World's Religions, in Chicago (1993), the interfaith gatherings that accompany such UN events as 'The Children Summit', 'The Earth Summit', 'The Social Summit', etc. are other 'time signals'. They point to the fact that if all life is interconnected, and all peoples are of God's concern, and if we are co-workers with God in the task of healing the earth and the life of all its people, then we should have a larger vision of what is 'ecumenical', both in scope and in our understanding of partners and co-workers in the ecumenical movement. It is not a call to establish that 'all religions are the same', or an admission that religious communities have no specific witness to offer. It is rather our preparedness to be more willing than before to be more involved than before in more of what God is doing among us.

We do have the option to stay with a tribal god, with a narrow understanding of salvation history, to define our purpose as seeking our own unity, and to see the rest of the world as misguided until we have shown them the road. As an ecumenical movement, we can insist that our deeply divided situation, which we have been unable to overcome in 70 years of conversations, is still the 'sign' of the coming unity of humankind. In a world that is falling apart by violence and war, we can continue to insist that we have been 'called out' and that the answer to the problems of the world is for everyone to believe as we do and to become part of our community.

I am only too aware that this is a caricature, and that in reality what Christians believe in is more complex and more nuanced. But it is a helpful way to speak about what the 'wider ecumenism' is calling us out of. It is a way to say that the new ecumenism is not a loss of 'confidence in the gospel', as Newbigin would describe it, but a new 'confidence in God' that comes from our rootedness in the gospel. It may not be within the 'logic of mission' of a past era, but it is certainly within the 'logic of the kingdom' for our day. It is the recovery of the pilgrim character of the church; its eyes are fixed not only on what God has done, but also on what God is doing and intends to do.

In September 1998, the World Council of Churches will meet in its Eighth Assembly in Harare, Zimbabwe, also to mark its Jubilee, the fiftieth year of its founding. One of the most significant processes of preparation for the assembly is a study process on 'The common understanding and vision' of the World Council of Churches, which seeks to discern the vision and ministry to which the council is being called within an ecumenical movement that has been impacted both by what has happened in the life of the churches and by so many significant events, radical changes and the phenomenal developments in fields of science, technology and communications over the past 50 years.

Interreligious dialogue is one of these impacts. In 1980, Cantwell Smith spoke of it as a 'small current that has begun to flow around and through the Christian church'. And then he added the warning:

It is a current which, although we are only beginning to be aware of it, is about to become a flood that could sweep us quite away unless we can, through greatly increased consciousness of its force and direction, learn to swim in its special and mighty surge.[15]

The flood is here. Swim, we must!

Notes

1 This paper appeared in the *Ecumenical Review* 49.2 (1997), pp. 212–22.

2 W. A. Visser 't Hooft, *Has the Ecumenical Movement a Future?* (Belfast: Christian Journals Limited, 1974), p. 30.

3 Stanley J. Samartha, 'Contact, controversy and communication', *Indian Journal of Theology* 17 (1968), p. 25. Quoted by Eeuwout Klootwijk, *Commitment and Openness: The Interreligious Dialogue and Theology of Religions in the Work of Stanley J. Samartha* (The Netherlands: Boeken-centrum, 1992), p. 62.

4 For the full report on 'Seeking community' and the dialogue debate see David M. Paton (ed.), *Breaking Barriers, Nairobi 1975: The Official Report of the Fifth Assembly of the World Council of Churches, Nairobi, 23 November–10 December, 1975* (Geneva: WCC, 1976), pp. 70–85.

5 *Guidelines on Dialogue with People of Living Faiths and Ideologies* (Geneva: WCC, 1990 (4th printing)), p. 11. For the full report of the consultation that brought together the contending parties at the Nairobi Assembly to agree on the 'Guidelines' later adopted by the Central Committee see Stanley J. Samartha (ed.), *Faith in the Midst of Faiths: Reflections on Dialogue in Community* (Geneva: WCC, 1977).

6 David Gill (ed.), *Gathered for Life: Official Report. VI Assembly, World Council of Churches, Vancouver, Canada, 24 July–10 August 1983* (Geneva: WCC, 1983), p. 40.

7 The English versions of *My Neighbour's Faith and Mine* and *The Bible and People of Other Faiths* were published by WCC, Geneva. For the report *From Baar I to Baar II* see *Current Dialogue* 26 (June 1994).

8 See Lesslie Newbigin, *The Gospel in a Pluralist Society* (Geneva: WCC, and Grand Rapids: Eerdmans, 1989). The chapters include 'The logic of election', pp. 80–8, 'The logic of mission', pp. 116–27, 'No other name', pp. 155–70, and 'Confidence in the gospel', pp. 242–4, all of which are attempts to reinstate in a pluralist context some of the traditional pillars on which the mission theology was built. On the question of the road, Newbigin affirms:

As a human race we are on a journey and we need to know the road. It is not true that all roads lead to the top of the mountain. There are roads that lead over the precipice. In Christ we have been shown the road. We cannot treat that knowledge as a private matter for ourselves. It concerns the whole human family … (p. 183)

9 Visser 't Hooft, *Has the Ecumenical Movement a Future?*, pp. 73–5.

10 Quoted here from *Dialogue with People of Living Faiths: Minutes of the Sixth Meeting of the Working Group* (March 1985) (Geneva: WCC, 1985), p. 27.

11 *Faith and Order, Louvain 1971: Study Reports and Documents* (Faith and Order paper no. 59; Geneva: WCC, 1971), p. 191.

12 Konrad Raiser, *Ecumenism in Transition: A Paradigm Shift in the Ecumenical Movement?* (Geneva: WCC, 1991), p. 86.

13 Ibid., pp. 54–9.

14 Ibid., p. 86.

15 Wilfred Cantwell Smith, 'The Christian in a religiously plural world' in John Hick and Brian Hebblethwaite (eds), *Christianity and Other Religions* (Glasgow: Collins, 1980), p. 87.

2

The Christian Trinity: paradigm for pluralism?

Gavin D'Costa

And the Lord appeared to him [Abraham] by the oaks of Mamre, as he
sat at the door of his tent in the heat of the day. He lifted up his eyes
and looked, and behold, three men stood in front of him. When he saw
them, he ran from the tent door to meet them, and bowed himself to
the earth, and said, 'My lord, if I have found favour in your sight, do
not pass by your servant. Let a little water be brought, and wash your
feet, and rest yourselves under the tree, while I fetch a morsel of bread,
that you may refresh yourselves, and after that you may pass on – since
you have come to your servant.' So they said, 'Do as you have said.'
And Abraham hastened into the tent to Sarah, and said, 'Make ready
quickly three measures of fine meal, knead it, and make cakes.' And
Abraham ran to the herd, and took a calf, tender and good, and gave it
to the servant, who hastened to prepare it. Then he took curds, and
milk, and the calf which he had prepared, and set it before them; and
he stood by them under the tree while they ate.

  They said to him, 'Where is Sarah your wife?' And he said, 'She is in
the tent.' The Lord said, 'I will surely return to you in the spring, and
Sarah your wife shall have a son.' And Sarah was listening at the tent
door behind him. Now Abraham and Sarah were old, advanced in age;
it had ceased to be with Sarah after the manner of women. So Sarah
laughed to herself, saying, 'After I have grown old, and my husband is
old, shall I have pleasure?' The Lord said to Abraham, 'Why did Sarah
laugh, and say, "Shall I indeed bear a child, now that I am old?" Is
anything too hard for the Lord? At the appointed time I will return to
you, in the spring, and Sarah shall have a son.' But Sarah denied,
saying, 'I did not laugh'; for she was afraid. He said, 'No, but you did
laugh.'[1] (RSV)

My unsystematic reflections are based on two images of the Trinity[2]
which seem to me to raise some profound questions concerning Christian 'negotiation'[3] with the Other. Both images deal with the question of
the Trinity in relation to Other religious traditions, although otherness
takes on fluid meanings, as we shall see. The first image is the fifteenth-

century icon from the Russian Orthodox painter Andrei Rublev, *The Trinity*. It raises the question of our making sense of God's presence to the Other and how we, as Christians, deal with this. Issues regarding negation, domestication, appropriation and transformation are raised, but not entirely resolved. The second image, which takes us into the modern period, is that of the Roman Catholic Indian artist Jyoti Sahi's beautiful painting, *The Word Made Flesh*. This painting keeps many of the previous issues afloat, but changes the context from Israel to Indian religions, thereby raising new sets of problems. In my commentary I shall range over a number of disparate but related issues suggesting only further avenues of exploration, rather than conclusions.

Andrei Rublev's The Hospitality of Abraham *or* The Old Testament Trinity *or* The Trinity[4]

There is some humour in this icon circulating under three names, but there is also a rather remarkable theological point concealed here. Rublev's *Trinity* is in fact the allegorical or iconic[5] representation of the three persons of the Trinity via the account of Abraham's and Sarah's meeting of three men/angels by the oaks of Mamre, in Genesis 18.[6] The first title (*The Hospitality of Abraham*) apparently respects the integrity of the story, but remains closed to any further signification. At one level it is a static reading of Hebrew scripture.[7] The second title (*The Old Testament Trinity*) already reveals a Christian theological rereading – in fact not unlike the rereading or renaming that takes place within the text itself: in the light of their transformative meeting with God, Abram becomes Abraham, Sar'ai changes to Sarah (Genesis 17:5, 15).[8] This hermeneutical rereading is inscribed within the 'New Testament' in relation to the 'Old', and always bears within it the terrifying possibility (not necessity) of the Marcionite extinction of the Jews. We must also keep in mind that Rublev's work takes place in the context of what Ouspensky calls the 'heresy of the Judaizers', those Christian reforming movements that denied the divinity of Christ and consequently the reality of the Trinity.[9] Interestingly, in God's renaming of Abram and Sar'ai there is transformation, but no extinction; however, renaming is not without specific cost, demand and sacrifice.[10]

The third title (*The Trinity*) represents an even deeper transformative re-presentation whereby Rublev apparently removes traces of the Genesis story (Abraham and Sarah, the various foods on the table)[11] to allow the story to be luminously more than itself, more than a *vestige* of the Trinity. It becomes a holy icon, inviting us into participation with the inner Trinitarian life of God. One might even call it an eschatological rereading of the Genesis story whereby our fractured histories are glimpsed, as it were, from God's point of view. But Rublev, we can be sure, would not have fallen into idolatry at exactly its most tempting moment.[12]

But let me return to the narrative of Genesis 18 which allows us to glimpse, *before the incarnation of the Son, but only through the incarnation of the Son*, and this is all important, the presence and absence of the triune God. The dialectics of this process are germane to the topic under consideration. Such allegorical or analogical readings are replete within the early church and could allow contemporary Christians to consider one possible form of relationship and negotiation with narratives from other traditions.[13] This happens in different contexts: conversions to Christianity, mission to others and the many other forms of negotiated encounters. Each context would demand different readings. (I have already alluded to the terrifying possibility of the destruction of the Other within this process whereby other religions are destroyed in their encounter with Christianity, but I would also want tentatively to suggest that Trinitarian reality profoundly contests this possibility.[14])

Abraham and Sarah already represent the beginnings of the covenant community (Genesis 17:2–21), people in relationship, and this relationship is by no means passive. In Genesis 18 Abraham initiates the communing together, though even here something is already required of him: 'if I have found favour in your sight, do not pass by your servant' (18:3 – all citations from RSV). Abraham and Sarah are deeply hospitable to their guests who are strangers, in typical near-Eastern fashion – and Westermann reminds us that this tradition also held that 'The stranger comes from another world and has a message from it'.[15] Hebrews 13:2 tellingly recalls the necessity of hospitality, echoing Genesis 18: 'Do not neglect to show hospitality to strangers, for thereby some have entertained angels unawares', or, even as with Matthew 25:40, they have attended to God in their attending to strangers. Hence, Rublev's depiction of the mutual sharing and self-giving within the Trinity *actually reconfigures* the story of Abraham and Sarah's 'giving' and shows both their immense generosity – and their lack of imagination, their disbelief in the radical impossible 'giving' which is God's giving, symbolized in the gift of a son to Sarah who is barren. This gift prefigures the Son, Jesus, who comes forth from a different context of barrenness, a virgin's womb, and who marks the deepening of the covenant with Abraham and Isaac.[16]

This transformative relationship between the primary narrative (Genesis 18) and its Trinitarian rereading is also enacted upon the physical elements constituting Abraham's and Sarah's generosity. They bring before their guests the goodness of the earth (bread cakes, milk, curd and tender calf). In Rublev's icon these are transformed, as in the

Eucharistic offertory, into the Eucharistic cup, lying central on the table between the three figures. The gift is transformed into eternal Gift, the Eucharist is the continual self-giving of God's life. So Rublev sees in Abraham and Sarah not only the foundation of the church, but in their bringing forth the fruits of the earth (as good stewards of the gifts given them) they prefigure the Eucharistic return, eternal life in the life of God.

To return to the gift – Isaac, we find in this narrative that God's presence is creative promise, his presence is fecundity, the bringing of hope beyond human resources but, importantly, not without the co-operation and creative response by human resources.[17] Abraham is 100 years old, Sarah 90, and it is little wonder that she laughs (18:12) as did Abraham earlier (17:17) when the promise of new birth is made. As an aside, Vawter's reading of the laughter – laughed (*yiṣḥaq*) is a wordplay on the name Isaac – is interesting in suggesting that their actions, without knowing it, anticipate that which is hidden to them in the present.[18] Such a reading further supports the type of exegesis that Rublev's icon constructs. But the gift of Isaac, this promise, is not without further purpose for it allows the even greater gift of God's love to be established with his covenanted people: 'I have chosen him [Abraham], that he may charge his children and his household after him to keep the way of the Lord by doing righteousness and justice' (18:19).[19]

I want to suggest that Rublev's depiction of the Trinity is deeply sensitive to the *deep patterns* within the story and that by contemplating the icon one is invited into a profound rereading of Genesis 18, which, rather than erasing the economic narrative in Genesis, reads it within the light of another narrative, the church of Jesus Christ, centred around the Eucharistic table, participating in the life of the triune God. My main contention is that *neither narrative is quite the same after this negotiation, nor should nor could it be*. Let me elaborate a little – and here of course I cannot speak for those within the Jewish community, although I'd be most grateful if they cared to respond to my comments. (An avenue that opens up here is an engagement with Jewish commentaries on Genesis 18 to further the negotiation that has already been carried out here.)

Rublev reconfigures the hospitality, the generosity and the faith of Abraham and Sarah as deeply nourishing and prophetic, for in its patterns of action (e.g. meal-giving, incredulity at God's 'giving', plead-ing for 'righteousness and justice' even to the point of getting God to budge (18:22–33)) it displays both the initiative of and response to the living presence of the Trinitarian God. (We might well remember this when turning to questions of ethics in other religions.) All these pat-terns of action are in fact taken up, reflected, questioned and recast within the Trinitarian life of God, renegotiating otherwise familiar texts to us. Meal-giving prefigures the sharing of the eternal life of God in the Eucharist. Incredulity at God's giving is surpassed and now takes the shape of the Son and Spirit within the icon: God's gracious gifts to us of himself. And Abraham's concern for righteousness and justice is evoked in the wood of the Cross via the oak at Mamre at the top off-centre of the icon. It is gently curved to mimic the movement of the body of Jesus towards the Father, who in the Cross justifies the wicked and unrighteous and brings salvation to sinners. He brings new life – the fingers point towards the cup. In this sacrifice he returns to the Father – notice the movement of exchange established by Jesus' eyes tenderly looking at the Father while his body faces the other way, towards the Spirit. He returns so that the gift of the Spirit can be given (John 7:39). In this negotiation with Genesis 18, Rublev's own Trinitarian iconic narrative is transformed as well as Genesis 18. Neither remains the same. However, the icon also raises some difficult questions.

Does Rublev's *Trinity* represent anything other than an old-style fulfilment theology? Put bluntly: Israel is nothing but a prefigurement of the church, and worse still, the occlusion of Abraham and Sarah from the Genesis narrative (despite the first title: *The Hospitality of Abraham*) is indicative of the potential genocidal logic in fulfilment theology. (One should also note the double effacement of Sarah, from representation and title.) The inclusion of Sarah and Abraham in the Russian Novgorod sixteenth-century depiction of the Trinity makes for an interesting comparison, although I do not think it entirely responds to the problem raised. (In this respect it would be interesting to explore the 'visibility' of Judaism in fifteenth-century Russia and the extent of anti-Jewish theology in the Russian church. The fact that Christian heretical groups were called 'Judaizers' is only significant in part.) The question will not and should not go away. It must *remain in tension* with the positive view I have been advancing, whereby the icon can be seen to reinterpret history from a Trinitarian perspective without distorting or effacing that history but indeed transforms it and itself in that process of rereading. The process of rereading is of course never complete.

Another related issue, which runs beyond the context of Jewish–Christian relations, concerns the process of rereadings which takes place within any negotiation. To stick for the moment with written 'scripture', is it not inevitable that while Christians should listen to and learn from how others practise and interpret their scripture, Christian readings and negotiation with such texts will sometimes seem like gross misreadings? Can this be avoided, if Christian theology is governed by a Trinitarian grammar, even if ironically, *this grammar is there precisely to guard against idolatry, against closure*, when we come to the question of God? Put bluntly, who 'owns' scriptures? Rublev's depiction alerts us to the fact that Genesis 18 constantly signifies more than itself, significations that may be resisted by some interpretative communities, but not by others. Judaism, Christianity and Islam are already part of that difficult intra-inter-textual set of networks whereby each one's sacred scripture belongs in part to the other and is often interpreted in deeply incompatible ways. One might even ask: Are these the same texts any more?[20] Without wishing to condemn myself, one might also see this issue operative in art, especially in relationship to the icon, which has recently become an item of popular capitalist consumerism in contrast to its sacred function within its generative communities.[21]

Jyoti Sahi's The Word Made Flesh

Rublev, as with orthodox Christianity, presupposes that the 'Old' Testament, the Hebrew scriptures, is part of Christianity's heritage. Put another way, the Word was made flesh within a very specific cultural-religious context, that of Judaism. Hence, Christianity in its inception was a process of rereading, reinterpretation and negotiation with the Jewish culture out of which it arose in response to the triune God.[22] And in this rereading, there were plural readings of Judaism, some deeply negative to the heretical point of Marcion, and some very positive to the problematic point of Ebionitism. This restless dialectic continued into Hellenistic culture which formed the crucible out of which Christians negotiated their own identity in response to what became the great creedal profession in a triune God. These negotiations carried no single assessment of the religious cultures within which Christianity lived and formed a part, but the only point I want to make is that *implicitly such assessment was part of the logic of learning to confess God as Father, Son and Spirit within these cultures.*[23]

Not surprisingly, some modern Christians, faced with the deeply spiritual cultures of Asia, have had to learn anew to practise, understand and construct their faith. If the Word was made flesh within a Jewish culture, the church, the body of Christ, is constantly being enfleshed within Asian culture. As before, there are very different reactions to the problems of pluralism, in part mirroring the early church. For example, Nestorian Syrian Christianity has developed for most of its history in splendid isolation from the Hindu culture within which it lived in South India, or we can find certain evangelical wholesale rejections of everything Hindu which bear some analogy to Marcionism, or, in contrast, various indigenous experimentations which have had the charge 'Hindu Christianity' levelled at them, which

may bear analogy with Ebionitism.[24] I now turn to Jyoti Sahi's Trinitarian painting of the *Word Made Flesh* to develop the discussion set in
motion by Rublev.

Rublev should in part be interpreted by various rules followed by
iconographers, although to limit the power of his art according to such
strictures would indeed be reductive. Sahi provides a slightly different
case, for his art deeply engages with a complex, fluid mixture of Indian
folk symbols, Jungian psychology and gospel stories, and does not
follow in a long tradition of Indian Christian art with clear rules of
representation. To begin to interpret his work is already a deep engagement with Indian folk culture made up of Hindu, Buddhist and Muslim
elements – although I shall only concentrate on the Hindu elements. In
this respect, once more as with Rublev, we find that Trinitarian confession *both binds and releases the artist to engage and negotiate with Other
religious cultures*. For Sahi, of course, as an Indian, this 'other' in the
form of symbols is already part of his 'own' make-up, as well as part of
the deep psychic shared life with thousands of non-Christian Indians.
Hence, in this section I will simply offer a commentary on some of the
forces at play in this Indian Trinitarian depiction, drawing heavily on
Sahi's work concerning Indian folk symbols, while not being constrained by his writings, none of which explicitly addresses the painting
under consideration.[25] Genesis 18, so to speak, is replaced by Indian
symbolic 'texts' in this negotiation, this re-presentation.

At one level the painting depicts the child being nourished by the
mother tenderly enfolding, in a graceful circular fashion, the suckling
infant. Her form is constituted by circular movements, almost like the
petals of a flower, which play with and echo the huge circular earth,
egg, womb, moon (sun/Son) within which the image is framed. Her
colour is the orange kavi of the holy person within the Indian tradition,
not the royal blue of Western depiction, and this colour also infuses the
infant. Intersecting from above there is a shape much like the dove of
the Holy Spirit that sweeps over, perhaps gently kissing, the Virgin's
neck, breathing life into the Word that she nourishes in her arms and by
her breasts. The curves of the dove create a rhythmic dance of forms
between Mary, child, the Spirit and the womb-earth-egg-moon, which
is heightened by a crescent-shaped moon near the neck of the dove.
Straight forms are rejected in this cosmic dance, implying rejection of
linear logic and the rationalization of the mystery that besets modernity
– both Eastern and Western.[26] At the bottom of the picture we have what
could be the waters of creation, or the fires of life, or even the fingers or
hand of God the Father from which this creation of the Word and world
arises, is upheld and affirmed. This latter form is certainly not clear, and
this, I am sure, is intentional, for Sahi comments 'The child symbol is an

image, making visible the invisible, or, as he is known in Hindu myth, "Guha", born of the "secret place"'.[27] The Son is the visible image of the invisible Father, the source of all life. Sahi, like Rublev, transcends the specific context of engagement (one with Genesis, the other with Indian religious symbols) so that most Christians (Indian or not), I would imagine, could see the gospel drama, the Word made flesh, being re-enacted in the painting. I shall also show how death and resurrection and church are also implicit.

However, at another level Sahi's picture is *entirely* constructed out of Indian religious symbols and, in so being, sets in motion a complex negotiation between different cultures and religions without any attempt at resolution. The moon, for instance, plays a central part in female fertility symbolism, closely related to its three stages (ascendant, full and receding), which in turn is related to the three-headed god/dess of the Indus Valley and prototype of Shiva, the god of creation.[28]

Aum, a sacred syllable used as a mantra in meditation. It symbolizes the three worlds, the three states of consciousness, the three *Vedas*, the past, present and future.

The moon is also an emblem of the sacred sound '*Om*' or '*Aum*'. The Sanskrit form of the word *Aum* indeed forms the shape of the dove, and its construction out of three crescents recalls both the lunar fertility and the Hindu *trimurti*: Brahma, Vishnu and Shiva (creator, preserver and destroyer). *Aum* is also said to be the eternal syllable out of which all arises and dissolves. The *Chandogya Upanishad* (2.23, 2–3) and the *Taittiriya Upanishad* (1, 8) assign the origin of language to Prajapati, from whose meditation arose the threefold knowledge (the three *Vedas*). From his meditation on them arose the three syllables: *bhur*, *bhavah* and *svar* (earth, atmosphere and sky), from which then originated the sacred syllable *Aum*, which co-ordinates all speech and represents the totality of the world.[29] The Spirit's role in creation, of both the world and Word, mediated through such complex symbols, allows the *feminine, bisexual or transsexual aspect of the Spirit* to be brought into form. The creation of the world by the Word is thereby mediated for Sahi through the fissures of this rich Indian tradition. But rather than my painting with such broad brush strokes, let me focus further on a single aspect of the painting concerning the feminine aspect of divine creativity.

The placing of the maternal form at the semicentre resonates deeply with Indian folk symbolism. To quote from Sahi:

> The world-process, known in India as samsara, is thought of as feminine. Between this world-process and the all-transcendent Father there is an eternal dialectic. In the highly developed metaphysics of the later medieval schools, the term adhara, meaning support, container, is supplied to the feminine, as opposed to adheya, meaning that which is to be supported, meaning here the masculine principle. Thus, although the feminine according to one viewpoint is understood as the relative, maya, seen in a different way it is the container of all that can be known, the very substance of all that is (sati).[30]

Certain recent Hindu 'liberation' movements have also tried to recover this feminine dimension from within the tradition, and in the conjunction of Mary with this stream of Hindu thought, as one central image of the painting, it poses a question to predominantly male-Western-theological thought forms about the suppressed and domesticated/dominated feminine, the source of life, the 'Mother'.[31] (Too often, even in some strands of Trinitarian thought – which tend towards subordinationism or modalism – the Father reigns alone, primary and aloof.) Here, Sahi's engagement with the Other requires a profound rethinking via Mary of the nature of the divine Trinity that he has inherited. In choosing not to represent the 'Father' as 'male' or 'person', Sahi creates symbolic space for reconsidering divine creativity in terms of female imagery which pulses through Indian religious folk symbolism. The theme of creation as a Trinitarian event is already configured through the use of the *Aum* symbol as noted above, but it is also negotiated through Sahi's reference to Genesis and its refiguring by St John in his prologue. The Spirit hovers over the waters (Genesis 1:2), giving birth to creation (echoing the Hindu myth of the cosmic egg, the *Hiranyagarbha*, coming forth from the churning of the oceans), and this is then also read through John's Gospel whereby the Word, by whom God created the world (John 1:3), is now made flesh in the incarnation (John 1:14).

A further interesting feature here concerns the breast-feeding of the infant. Mary's breasts are swelling and fecund, and here Sahi echoes the Indian feminine:

> The Indian feminine figure is depicted with swelling breasts. This again is thought to show her overflowing fertility, rather than her specific relation to a child whom she is feeding. It is almost as if the Indian feminine figure has been abstracted beyond any personal relationship,

which is the intention behind the highly personalized depictions of the mother and child images of Christian art. For here the woman is the all-embracing principle of nature, and even the milk that fills her breasts is described as 'the essence of water and of the plants'.[32]

In depicting the child suckling, in a stroke Sahi employs the richness and universalism of Indian symbolic language (the all-embracing principle of nature with overflowing fertility) and fuses it with the particularity of personal love between Mary and Jesus – and the Holy Spirit. But the power of this fusion also shows that being Christ-like is also deeply feminine; it is the nourishing of the body, the tender glory in God's creation seen in Mary. The church is often represented as Mary, mother in Western art and theology, and the church's mission is to nourish a Christ-likeness through the grace of the Spirit. In another context, the late Middle Ages, Caroline Walker Bynum has brilliantly explored the role of breast-feeding and its implications for the female-ness of Christ and the notion of the church as nourishing mother.[33] Sahi's painting opens many similar possibilities for exploring various feminine roles for the church called to serve creation through love, nourishment and 'divine' creativity. I say 'divine' creativity because this is perhaps suggested in the Holy Spirit intersecting the globe shape, the cosmic egg, and the dark chaos that throws into relief the miracle of creation. And why else are all these figures dancing with the movements of their circular shapes, if not taking part in the dance of creation – so often depicted in the beautiful dance of Shiva, Nataraja, the Lord of the Dance?[34]

But there is yet another important and dark, even ambiguous, echo in this breast-feeding depiction, one which touches upon the harrowing death (and resurrection) awaiting the infant, for it calls to mind the myth of Krishna who as a baby was at one time 'nurtured' by the demoness Putna who gave the babe her breast which was filled with poison. However, Krishna drank all the poison, in fact drained dry the demoness, who was thereby defeated. And this story in turn evokes the important myth of creation, where Shiva drinks the poison generated from the churning of the cosmic ocean (the bottom of the painting could be waves) to save the world from destruction. Is there a creative tension revealed here in relation to the story of the Son who takes unto himself the evil and sin of the world, and, in this action of self-immolation, begets and nourishes a new creation? Sahi comments on the Krishna and Shiva accounts: 'Both myths probably relate to an ancient concept of recreation by swallowing, but here food is given a negative value – as poison it cannot be absorbed, but has to be transformed through a ritual death.'[35] I'm not altogether convinced by Sahi's interpretation regarding the absorption of poison at this point, but already to the Indian mind we can see a rich set of associations being triggered regarding the relationship of this *istadevata*, Jesus, to the many popular gods. How is this one child related to the many other gods within Hinduism, many of whom have shared his childhood state? Sahi seems to suggest a deeper organic connection between the Word made flesh in Jesus and the creative power of the divine found within differing aspects of Hinduism embodied within different gods.[36] We are also faced with the question of the relationship of the Eucharistic food as sacrificial participation in the redeeming activity of God, in negotiated contrast with Shiva's sacrificial redemption and Krishna's too. And this question is profoundly a question about the place of the Christian church in Indian culture. Rublev's Eucharistic focus also shows, like Sahi, that Trinitarian language, worship and practice is generated within a community trying to participate in the divine life within a fractured and beautiful world which is God's creation. Sahi, however, allows for a more radical mutual transformation than is imagined by Rublev. God's Trinitarian richness is daringly and strikingly negotiated through the symbols of Indian religious folk art in a way partially analogous to the luminous reconfiguration of Genesis 18.

There are numerous issues that the painting raises, and I've only just started to trace one or two in relation to my concern with the Trinity and the Other. I must now draw to an end with some questions, keeping in mind our conversation with Rublev. Is Sahi guilty of the same imperializing tendency? Does he Christianize Indian folk symbols by utilizing them for his own purpose, thereby effacing their Otherness? From his writings – although we must let the image speak for itself – the answer is clearly 'no'. I happen to think that the image quite independently supports this. Sahi is Indian and the symbols he employs are 'Indian'. He is clear that they belong to the structures and cycles of village life and interestingly he reports that near Bangalore, where he lives, there are three villages of different religions (Hindu, Christian and Muslim) which all share the same folk symbolic culture which feeds differently into each tradition.[37] Hence, in the painting there is a real negotiation with these traditions which are his, but not his alone, a nourishing by and immersion in the waters of the Ganges, not Euphrates nor Jordan nor the Tiber, such that the Indian Trinitarian Christianity that emerges in this picture is a messy, complicated, yet beautiful and creative interaction with Indian religions.[38] There is, on the one hand, a disruption of the Western inheritance of Christian 'Trinitarianism' which I have alluded to regarding the feminine, and, on the other hand, a reconfiguration of a genuinely Indian Trinitarianism which both affirms and questions Indian culture and is transformed through this unfinished negotiation.

But if Sahi avoids the imperialistic charge, does he escape the syncret-
istic one from another wing of the Indian church? Put bluntly: If a
Hindu were to look at this painting would they recognize the differences between Hinduism and Christianity? Is the cosmic dance of Shiva
and the order of creation really analogous to the status of the created
order in Christianity? Is *Aum* really commensurate to the Holy Spirit?
Are Brahma, Vishnu and Shiva the same symbolically as Father, Son
and Spirit? (One might usefully compare the *trimurti*-trinity image at
the entrance to the late Bede Griffiths' ashram which makes the difference abundantly clear while not effacing relationship, by allowing the
three faces to emerge from the cross.) Are these differences occluded in
Sahi's work? Is Sahi, as his writings sometimes suggest, verging on
implying that the different traditions mediate the divine in different
ways; a kind of fashionable Western liberal pluralism advanced
recently by a number of theologians?[39] I raise this question, not to
answer it, but to show what is at stake when examining the extent to
which Trinitarian grammar may help us engage with the Other. One of
Sahi's points, I think, is that this Other is always also us, as well as
Other, and to lose either polarity is to fail to allow the Trinitarian
dynamic of difference in creative relation to flourish in our ecclesial and
subconscious lives.

Some hasty conclusions

What of these haunting images? I do not want to clutter their power by
even more words, but one point that they raise is that Christian
negotiation with the Other is not possible outside a Trinitarian dynamic
which is entrusted to the church. Looking at Rublev and Sahi we must
face the question about both preserving *difference* – Otherness – while
also engaging with this Other in *relationship*, relationship which is
always open to further negotiation. On the one hand effacement of the
Other always carries with it a violence against creation – most painfully
raised in Rublev's icon regarding the possibility of Christian anti-
Judaism and in Sahi's painting, namely the imperialism towards
Hinduism and the East. On the other hand, failing to relate creatively to
difference, Otherness, is also Christian violence against creation, for it
implies that God is not the God of all creation, that somehow God is
only at work in one small group of people. While this seems perfectly
possible, God help us if we were to identify ourselves as this small
group of people. Matthew 25 suggests that 'neither the rejection of Jesus
nor the receiving of his grace may readily be identifiable as such'.[40] As
was evident in Sahi's conflation of Genesis and John, God's creation is
a profoundly Trinitarian act and we cannot presume that God has left

himself without witness always and everywhere. Whether these two particular pictures have maintained this balance between Otherness and relatedness is one question; but that they raise this question is all important.

There are inevitably many neglected areas in this paper: politics and prayer, sex and violence, music and drama, sin and tragedy, animals and environment – to name a few. If Trinitarian life pervades creation, as the Trinitarian God is creator of all, then none of these issues can bypass Trinitarian mediation, although we cannot know in advance how the Trinity will 'look' in the process of these mediations. During such negotiation, we cannot predict what our practice, worship and theology will look like and we shall only be able to assess it retrospectively. And sometimes we will be deeply ashamed and terrified at the violence done to the Other – and, in this process, to ourselves. We can perhaps only dimly hope that, being drowned in the oceanic depths of God, as his currents and grace wash us up on shores that we no longer recognize we shall come to know that those shores have been shaped by him. We can perhaps only dimly pray that in learning to be ready to suffer like the mother giving birth, we might, with our neighbour, nourish the possibility of a new creation. We can perhaps only dimly trust that the endless mess that this whole process involves will not end in tragedy and loss – for Trinitarian life came through hopelessness and abandonment – but in kenotic surrender, endless, quite ridiculous love.

I am grateful for the helpful comments of Tina Beattie and Gerard Loughlin on a draft of this essay.

Notes

1 Genesis 18:1–15.
2 The images are reproduced on the front and back cover of this book.
3 Negotiation is perhaps preferable to dialogue. In another context, Graham Ward has convincingly argued that 'dialogue' tends to be framed within philosophical idealism, ignoring the problematic socio-political contexts of 'exchange'. He employs Derrida's term 'negotiation' as

[It] is more pragmatic and does not imply the *telos* of a truth to be understood. Negotiation suggests suspicion of intentionality (one's own and the other's); it suggests that each participant in any encounter comes heavily laden with presuppositions and previous contexts; it suggests that the movement in the transfer being performed is slippery and not necessarily progressive. Negotiation is the economy of textuality itself.

The Christian Trinity: paradigm for pluralism? 35

Graham Ward, *Barth, Derrida and the Language of Theology* (Cambridge: Cambridge University Press, 1995), p. 174; see also John Milbank's reflections on the liberal pluralist undergirdings of the term 'dialogue' in John Milbank, 'The end of dialogue' in Gavin D'Costa (ed.), *Christian Uniqueness Reconsidered* (New York: Orbis, 1990), pp. 174–91. Kenneth Surin's essay in the same collection also supports the point: 'A "politics of speech" ', ibid., pp. 192–212. Talal Asad, *Genealogies of Religion: Discipline and Reasons of Power in Christianity and Islam* (Baltimore: Johns Hopkins University Press, 1993), also makes clear (from a Muslim point of view?) that dialogue is too uncritical a term in view of the politics of encounter.
4 Painted by Rublev for the monastery of the Trinity and St Sergius, probably between 1408 and 1425, now in the Tretyakov Gallery, Moscow. Technically, it should be called *The Old Testament Trinity* in comparison with the two other forms of Orthodox Trinitarian depiction: the Paternity and the New Testament Trinity. See Leonid Ouspensky, *Theology of the Icon*, vol. 2 (New York: St Vladimir's Seminary Press, 1992), esp. pp. 262–73, 399–403. See also Leonid Ouspensky and Vladimir Lossky, *The Meaning of Icons* (New York: St Vladimir's Seminary Press, 1982), which contains more colour plates, and specifically on Rublev's *Trinity* see pp. 200–5. See also *Contemplating Icons: An Introduction to Icons and Prayer*, video (Slough, UK: St Paul Multimedia Productions, 1989) based on Victor Bakchine, *Introduction à la connaissance des icônes*.
5 See Raimundo Panikkar, *The Trinity and the Religious Experience of Man* (New York: Orbis, 1973), pp. 11–19, for a fascinating discussion of what he terms 'iconolatry' which could allow this discussion to develop very differently. See also Ouspensky, *Icon*, for the careful historical formulation of the difference between icon and idol. Jean-Luc Marion's use of such a distinction could perhaps be fruitfully related to the discussion. See his *God Without Being* (Chicago: Chicago University Press, 1991).
6 I leave aside the discussion of whether it was two or three angels or men or oaks or terebinths, whether verse 1a is original or not, and many other technical exegetical questions. See commentaries by Claus Westermann, *Genesis 12 – 36: A Commentary* (London: SPCK, 1986); Gerhard von Rad, *Genesis: A Commentary* (London: SCM, 3rd edn, 1972); and St Augustine, *The Trinity* (*The Fathers of the Church*, vol. 45; Washington, DC: Catholic University Press of America, 1963), 2.11–12. It is also worth comparing the startling commentary on Abraham and Isaac provided by Kierkegaard, and Erich Auerbach, *Mimesis: The Representation of Reality in Western Literature* (Princeton: Princeton University Press, 1953), ch. 1. Engaging with these brings us back to the scriptural texts afresh, engendered in a similar way by Trinitarian rereading.
7 Westermann, *Genesis*, reflects this in terms of his reductive historical-critical reading of the text, so that he exclaims: 'There is no way in which one can consider the present event an appearance of God, though the majority of exegetes speak of it in this way' (p. 275).
8 Von Rad, *Genesis*, while still constrained by historical-critical canons, is

more open to such rereadings: 'One is therefore rather inclined to think that Yahweh appeared in all three' (p. 204). Nevertheless, he says, 'The interpretation given by the early church that the trinity of visitors is a reference to the Trinity has been universally abandoned by recent exegesis' (p. 206). But 'recent' exegesis has moved on considerably since 1972; see for example Francis Watson (ed.), *The Open Text: New Directions for Biblical Studies* (London: SCM, 1993) and Anthony Thiselton, *New Horizons in Hermeneutics: The Theory and Practice of Transforming Biblical Reading* (London: HarperCollins, 1992).

9 See Ouspensky, *Icon*, p. 263. I say Marcionite because such rereadings of extinction are rightly deemed heretical. Rosemary Ruether makes it a necessity in her *Faith and Fratricide* (New York: Seabury Press, 1974); and see my argument against 'necessity' in 'One covenant or many covenants? Towards a theology of Christian–Jewish relations' in Robin Gill (ed.), *Readings in Modern Theology* (London: SPCK, 1995), pp. 173–85.

10 So although Abraham will know God's justice better than God admits (Genesis 18:22–32), he will not 'understand' it when called to sacrifice his son (Genesis 22).

11 Compare the inclusion of the cluttered table and Abraham and Sarah in *Old Testament Trinity*, Novgorod School, *c.* 1400 (Russian Museum, Leningrad). I am indebted to Lucy Tanner for allowing me to see her third-year undergraduate dissertation: 'The relationship between theology and art in the exploration of the Trinity' (Bristol University, 1994), which contained numerous images that I had not seen before.

12 This level is reflected in St Augustine's reading, *The Trinity*, note 6 above. However, this is not to say that it 'is' the immanent Trinity: 'it is not a representation of the Trinity itself, that is, of the three Persons of the Godhead, since in its essence the Godhead cannot be represented' (Ouspensky and Lossky, *Icons*, p. 203); see also Ouspensky, *Icon*, ch. 14 regarding the edicts of the Great Moscow Council of 1667 on the iconic rather than idolatrous representation of God. In the Orthodox tradition, represented by Lossky, following Gregory Palamas, the Godhead in itself is the darkness of unknowing; the 'energies' mediate Father, Son and Spirit. See Vladimir Lossky, *The Mystical Theology of the Eastern Church* (London: James Clarke & Co., 1968), esp. ch. 2, 'The divine darkness' and ch. 5, 'Uncreated energies'. One of the best introductions to Lossky is Rowan Williams, 'The via negativa and the foundations of theology: an introduction to the thought of V. N. Lossky' in Stephen Sykes and Derek Holmes (eds), *New Studies in Theology* (London: Duckworth, 1980), pp. 95–118.

13 See Andrew Louth, *Discerning the Mystery* (Oxford: Clarendon Press, 1983), for the early church's methods of exegesis, and Hans Frei, *The Eclipse of Biblical Narrative: A Study in Eighteenth and Nineteenth Century Hermeneutics* (New Haven, CT: Yale University Press, 1974), for the 'eclipse' of this type of reading.

14 I cannot attend to the socio-political implications of Trinitarian theo-

logy, and, although I have deep reservations, Jürgen Moltmann's *The Trinity and the Kingdom of God* (London: SCM, 1981) is surely central in alerting us to such implications. See also John Milbank, *Theology and Social Theory* (Oxford: Blackwell, 1990), which although underdeveloped in Trinitarian terms is deeply political.

15 Westermann, *Genesis*, p. 277. The cargo cults also worked on this principle, but with very different results.

16 This transformative rereading works both ways of course, for now we must reread Elizabeth and Mary's stories, which will in turn require a rereading of Sarah's story.

17 This telling should not obscure the duet story that follows in Genesis (18:16 – 19:21) whereby God is also judgement, so that fecundity cannot be viewed uncritically.

18 B. Vawter's commentary on Genesis in Reginald C. Fuller et al. (eds), *A New Catholic Commentary on Holy Scripture* (London: Nelson, 1969), pp. 166–205 (194). Karl-Josef Kuschel is interesting on Sarah's laughter and notes how Paul in Romans 4:19–21 fails to reinterpret the Sarah/Abraham narrative faithfully by not recognizing the drama of Genesis 17:7 (Abraham falling on his face in response to God, while at the same time laughing): see Karl-Josef Kuschel, *Laughter: A Theological Essay* (London: SCM, 1994), pp. 49–53. Freud's view of laughter can be tellingly employed here in terms of the dissonance encapsulated in such laughter. See S. Freud, *Jokes and the Relationship to the Unconscious* (1905) (Freud Library, vol. 6; Harmondsworth: Penguin, 1976).

19 See John Milbank, 'Can a gift be given?' in L. Gregory Jones and Stephen E. Fowl (eds), *Rethinking Metaphysics* (Oxford: Basil Blackwell, 1995), pp. 119–61, esp. 144–61, who argues in contrast to Derrida and Bourdieu who question the very possibility of 'gift'. Milbank locates gift within Trinitarian relationship.

20 This is the partial truth in Wilfred Cantwell Smith, *What Is Scripture?* (London: SCM, 1993), but Cantwell Smith does not take seriously the claims made within any interpretative community in deference to an allegedly general descriptive theory that he imposes upon all 'scriptures'.

21 The ownership of signs is a deeply political question, as is clear from the controversy concerning the representation of Picasso's paintings in the film about him by Merchant–Ivory.

22 One would have to qualify this statement, as there is considerable controversy regarding the status of the Trinity within the New Testament communities. But see Arthur Wainwright, *The Trinity in the New Testament* (London: SPCK, 1962), and the interesting study by A. T. Hanson, *Jesus Christ in the Old Testament* (London: SPCK, 1965).

23 See Paul Hacker, *Theological Foundations of Evangelization* (St Augustin: Franz Steiner Verlag, 1980), ch. 2; Henri de Lubac, *The Church: Paradox and Mystery* (Shannon: Ecclesia Press, 1969), ch. 4; and the very helpful monograph by C. Saldhana, *Divine Pedagogy: A Patristic View of Non-*

Christian Religions (Rome: LAS, 1984). For understanding Christian confession of Trinity as a learning of grammar, see the most helpful work by Nicholas Lash, 'Considering the Trinity', *Modern Theology* 2.3 (1986), pp. 183–96; idem, *Believing Three Ways in One God: A Reading of the Apostles' Creed* (London: SCM, 1992); and Rowan Williams, 'Trinity and revelation', *Modern Theology* 2.3 (1986), pp. 197–212.

24 For an excellent history of Christianity in India see Stephen Neill, *A History of Christianity in India: The Beginnings to AD 1707* (Cambridge: Cambridge University Press, 1984). For the complex and pluralist state of theological reflection today see M. Amaladoss et al. (eds), *Theologizing in India* (Bangalore: Theological Publications in India, 1981). On indigenization in India and some problems of methodology see my 'Inculturation, India and other religions: some methodological reflections', *Studia Missionalia* (Rome: Gregorian University Press) 44 (1995), pp. 121–47.

25 See Sahi's study *The Child and the Serpent: Reflection on Popular Indian Symbols* (London: Routledge & Kegan Paul, 1980). See also on Indian symbolism Heinrich Zimmer, *Myths and Symbols in Indian Art and Civilization* (Princeton, NJ: Princeton University Press, 1963); Stella Kramrisch, *The Art of India* (London: Phaidon, 1965); W. D. O'Flaherty, *Ascetism and Eroticism in the Mythology of Siva* (Oxford: Oxford University Press, 1975).

26 Sahi, *Child*, pp. 8–11.

27 Sahi, *Child*, p. 103.

28 See Sahi, *Child*, chs 8 and 9. All diacritical marks have been omitted from transliterated Sanskrit words.

29 See H. Zimmer, *Philosophies of India* (Bollingen Series, XXVI; Princeton, NJ: Princeton University Press, 1951), pp. 372–8. There is a considerable difference in the understanding and use of *Aum* within the Hindu tradition. The Christian interpolation enters yet one more, but related, reading.

30 Sahi, *Child*, p. 113.

31 See Bharat Dogra, *Towards a Liberation Theology of Hinduism* (publication details not given), which reads the *Ramayana* in terms of liberation, including feminist liberation in Dalit theology. Of course, feminists within the West have also raised similar issues, but the differences here should not be minimized, especially because of the different dynamics inherent within the cultural symbolic traditions. See also Sahi, *Child*, chs 3, 9 and 10, which in turn are also heavily dependent on Jung. The Orthodox and Roman Catholic traditions have kept this Marian dimension alive, with various ambiguous consequences: see respectively Lossky, *Mystical Theology of the Eastern Church*, pp. 140–4, 193–5; Hans Urs von Balthasar, *Mary for Today* (Slough: St Paul's Publications, 1987). For a recent inspiring Roman Catholic reappropriation of Mary, see also Tina Beattie, *Rediscovering Mary: Insights from the Gospel* (London: Burns & Oates, 1995). See also Marina Warner, *Alone of All Her Sex: The Myth and the Cult of the Virgin Mary* (London: Picador, 1990).

32 Sahi, *Child*, p. 114.

33 Caroline Walker Bynum, *Fragmentation and Redemption: Essays on Gender and the Human Body in Medieval Religion* (New York: Zone Books, 1991), esp. chs 6 and 3.

34 This is the term applied to Shiva when he performs the Tandava dance, representing the continuous creation, maintenance and destruction of the universe, and indicates the perfect balance within the divine between life and death. It must be said that 'creation' within Hinduism and Christianity poses very different problems and is quite fundamentally different, but not without overlaps. See Julius Lipner, 'The Christian and Vedantic theories of originative causality: a study in transcendence and immanence', *Philosophy East and West* 28.11 (1978), pp. 53–68.

35 Sahi, *Child*, p. 38. But see Bynum, *Fragmentation*, pp. 139–42, 186–8, for an interesting examination of consumption, food and Eucharist in relation to somatic identification with Christ.

36 See Sahi's own comments on this: 'all concepts of this child god flow in and out of each other': *Child*, p. 3.

37 Sahi, *Child*, pp. 10–11.

38 I have concentrated mainly on the Hindu, but Sahi draws upon Buddhist and Muslim traditions as well. For instance, in the present painting there is important light thrown on the use of the moon and Hindu symbolic mathematics from the Buddhist notion of *sunya* – see *Child*, pp. 104–5, 196. It would also be interesting to reflect on Sahi in the light of the Trinitarian explorations of Indian Roman Catholics such as Swami Abhishiktananda and Jules Monchanin.

39 John Hick, *An Interpretation of Religion* (London: Macmillan, 1988), being one of the best known.

40 Rowan D. Williams, 'Postmodern theology and the judgement of the world' in Frederick B. Burnham (ed.), *Postmodern Theology: Christian Faith in a Pluralist World* (San Francisco: HarperCollins, 1989), pp. 92–112 (p. 97).

3

Feminism: the missing dimension in the dialogue of religions

Ursula King

Introductory clarifications

I wish to examine the important theme of interfaith encounter and interreligious dialogue from the perspective of women. Whereas the wider experience of interfaith encounter has a long history, much of what we understand today by 'interreligious dialogue' has come about through the initiative and influence of different Christian groups. Interreligious dialogue thus has historical roots in earlier colonial and missionary activities and events. Like all of these it is also, at the same time, linked to strongly established patriarchal structures and andro-centric modes of thought, as I hope to show.

Without denying the economic and political motives behind the Christian missionary enterprise of the past, it is important to realize that the historical experience of worldwide missions undertaken by differ-ent Christian churches contributed to the gradual emergence of a growing global consciousness among people in the West. This also included a rising awareness of the spiritual challenge posed by differ-ent religious world-views. In her essay on 'Fundamentalism and the control of women' Karen McCarthy Brown[1] has pointed to the sig-nificance of the theological task Christian missions faced:

> If religion is the repository of the symbols that orient us within the
> world, then, as our world expands, so must our religions' ability to
> comprehend that world and to place us – individuals and communities
> – meaningfully within it. But Western Christianity, arguably the first
> religion to face the challenge of developing a truly global world-view,
> proved unequal to the task.[2]

The point made here is important. In today's situation Christianity cannot meet the spiritual challenge of our time on its own. The global situation, reflected at regional and local levels, is marked by an explo-sive experience of religious, cultural, social and political pluralism. This situation impacts differently on different religions. It can have deeply disruptive effects and lead to tension and strife, but it also has an enormous potential for good, for a deepening of encounter and the collaboration between people of different religious commitments.

Much has been written on the theological challenges of religious pluralism already, but it is important to go on examining both the theological and political dimensions of the interrelationship between pluralism and different religions. The relationship between ethnic and cultural pluralism in different societies and the different religions present in each society occurs not simply in a one-dimensional context, nor can this new situation be met by either theological or political reflections alone. The existence of this interrelationship itself calls for pluralistic answers – for diverse methods and approaches and a creative effort of critical self-reflection on the part of individuals and communities. From this perspective I should like to emphasize the need to enquire *religiously* into the meaning of religious pluralism. It is not simply a question of recognizing and respecting diversity, but we need to reflect on the consciously acknowledged existence of pluralism. This requires the creation and acceptance of a new grid of complexity which comes into existence through the relationships between the different constituent parts of a larger whole. All pluralism, but especially religious pluralism, has to be seen in a larger global context, and religious pluralism has to be understood as carrying ultimately *a spiritual significance.*

We have reached a new historical threshold in the history of the human species which includes the emergence of a new 'critical corporate consciousness' around the globe. Indications of this are found in several twentieth-century thinkers of different religious traditions who discern certain patterns and movements towards greater unity in the religious history of humankind. Wilfred Cantwell Smith is not alone in his assessment that the current 'shift from unawareness and insouciance to the new recognition of our global interdependence ... in spiritual matters'[3] sets us the challenging task of how we can meaningfully learn from each other in mutuality and trust. This certainly must include the possibility of mutual questioning and critique, but we must also be able to explore together the specific insights, moments of revelation and spiritual treasures which different religions have accumulated and handed down from one generation to the next, whereby the lives of countless people in the past and present have been nourished, strengthened and transformed.

It is undeniable that the growth of interreligious dialogue has created a new dynamic for religions and opened up new questions for theological and spiritual reflection. When immersing ourselves in the process of interreligious dialogue, we not only experience the extraordinary variety and richness of different historical and theological traditions, but we also come to recognize the deep injustices and wounds we have inflicted on each other. This is not only true in general, but it applies also to certain groups more than others, and foremost among them are women who, as half the human race, have been marginalized and oppressed in all religious traditions of historical time.

Thus one can legitimately ask whether, in spite of all the rich flowering of interreligious dialogue over recent years, the horizon of global ecumenism is still conceived of in terms that are too narrow; one must enquire whether the full potential of a 'new season of faith' can really come into its own as long as interreligious dialogue continues to include oppressive and exclusive aspects. Such narrowness is evident with regard to the marginalization, invisibility and exclusion of women, for wherever interreligious dialogue has developed, women seem to have had little part in it, at least at the official level. Proof for this is found in every single book on interfaith dialogue, religious pluralism, the theology of religions, or the 'wider ecumenism' of global interreligious encounter. If one's sensibility is attuned to these silences, the evidence of women's absence is further highlighted by the visual documentation of any interfaith meeting. One only has to look at the photographs of the meeting of religious leaders in Assisi or at those of any other official interfaith gathering to be shocked into the realization that all ecumenical gatherings, whether interdenominational or interreligious, are dominated almost exclusively by male representatives of the human race. Can these 'religious leaders' today still legitimately 'voice' the concerns of women and speak on their behalf, as if women could not speak for themselves?

This is constantly happening, while at the same time women from different faith communities are increasingly getting in touch with each other in order to share their experiences of oppression under the patriarchal structures of their religions and develop collaborative strategies of resistance and empowerment. They are also in dialogue with each other to share their visions of liberation, trying to work out together a new praxis for personal and social transformation. It is characteristic of religious feminism that it is not only an academic method which envisages *how* religions are *studied*, but it also embraces a new social and religious vision that affects *what* religion *is*, i.e. *how* religions are *lived and practised*.

Interreligious dialogue, as currently understood, practised and promoted in many parts of the world, particularly among Christians, is strongly marked by the absence of women. Nor have feminist writers on religion, when critiquing the patriarchal framework of different religions, paid much attention to the new developments in inter-religious dialogue circles. If one examines current interreligious activities, personnel and publications from a critical gender perspective, it is evident that, apart from a few, rare exceptions, feminism remains a missing dimension of dialogue. This could be substantiated by reference to numerous examples, such as the official dialogue activities of the World Council of Churches or those of the Vatican, or those of a new foundation such as the International Interfaith Centre in Oxford, England, or the various centennial celebrations of the 1893 World's Parliament of Religions organized in Bangalore, Chicago, and other places in 1993. Gender considerations are usually never an integral part of such organizations and events.

The same can be said about the numerous publications on inter-religious dialogue and religious pluralism. One has to have a feminist consciousness to notice the lacunae, the relative non-participation of women in this 'dialogue'. No references to women's contributions are to be found in either Marcus Braybrooke's historical directory of *Inter-Faith Organizations 1893–1979*[4] or in Francis Clark's *Interfaith Directory*,[5] and when edited works on interreligious dialogue contain a few contributions by women, such as Celia and David Storey's *Visions of an Interfaith Future*,[6] they are rarely written from a consciously feminist perspective.

But instead of assembling a great deal of cumulative evidence to prove that women's perspectives and contributions are always excluded, and that from a woman's perception much of interreligious dialogue might easily resemble what the French call 'un dialogue des sourds' (a dialogue of the deaf), I consider it more fruitful to raise some questions of a more theoretical nature regarding the mutual challenge of feminism and interreligious dialogue. In other words, I want to get away from the tacitly assumed 'inclusion' of women in the general discourse of dialogue and problematize the missing dimension of feminism in the practices and reflections of religions in dialogue. This procedure might contribute to a greater critical consciousness in this sphere and help us to enquire whether interreligious dialogue can become truly 'en-gendered' and thereby develop its own, new and original efforts in overcoming the oppression of women which has its deepest roots in religious symbols, structures, teachings and institutions.

The challenge of feminism for interreligious dialogue

First I want to clarify the understanding of interreligious dialogue on which my discussion is based. In North America reference is mostly made to 'interreligious dialogue' (Germans too speak about *inter-religiöser Dialog*, which shows that this notion is found elsewhere). In Britain people talk more of 'interfaith dialogue', thereby indicating perhaps that dialogue does not occur between religions *per se*, between religions as systems of beliefs and practices, but happens among people as a personal, existential engagement in the process of which the persons dialoguing with each other are touched on a deeper, more inward level. Their very understanding of faith comes into play; their entire world-view may be called into question or be enriched and transformed; and they may feel empowered to collaborate with people of other faiths to achieve common aims.

Of course, there are no persons in this world who are not gendered, and one has to ask *whether* the experience of interreligious dialogue is different for women than it is for men, and *how* a dialogue experience affects women as distinct from men. There can be no doubt that at present women are not appropriately and adequately represented in interreligious dialogue as a *collective endeavour* – they are more noted for their absence than their presence – and yet at a personal level, and in small groups, many women of different faiths are involved in inter-religious dialogue, participate in meetings and help to shape more links between members of different religious groups.

The first challenge of feminism to interreligious dialogue is thus one of women's official participation, their lack of *equal representation* and of the specific contribution of women's own voices. At present these are simply unheard and presumed to be included under whatever men have to say about dialogue. If one studies the dynamics of dialogue, the absence of women in the sense of either their marginalization or complete invisibility is another example of the patriarchal oppression of women. As much dialogue at the official level is carried out between 'religious leaders' – and such leaders are still by and large only male – it follows that women are excluded on the grounds of their sex. The official, visible representatives or 'spokesmen' of dialogue are literally always men, and thus men often find it difficult to listen to women in this context. I can remember an embarrassing occasion when, during an interreligious dialogue conference in an Asian country, visits to different religious communities were organized, and another woman and I decided that we should like to visit a particular religious group, which was quite a traditional one. The entire local congregation had turned out in full force, but for them to receive just two women delegates and no men was rather a shock. Another example was that of two distinguished religious scholars dialoguing with each other on spirituality, where one at least was adamant in not admitting a woman, however much experienced in meditation and interfaith encounters, to this exclusive male dialogue.

The challenge of gender is the challenge of *otherness* in a different guise, and it may be the most difficult one to accept for men in positions of religious leadership. To accept the 'other faith' is already recognized to be problematic, but this other faith is usually at least encountered through another man. Thus in interreligious dialogue woman is again *doubly other*: she is of *another* faith and a *different* gender, except where women of faith dialogue with each other.

Historically speaking, interreligious dialogue is a relatively recent concern, even more recent than the women's movement itself. The latter began near the beginning of the nineteenth century whereas the 'interfaith movement', as some describe it,[7] is in retrospect considered to have begun at the end of the century, with the historic meeting of people from different religions at the Chicago World's Parliament of Religions in 1893. Both the women's and the interfaith movements imply important historical changes at the social, political and economic level; both have a radical impact on the transformation of human consciousness at the individual and collective level; and both have a decisive role in the restructuring, or what has been called the 'reconception', of religion. An important observation to add here is the realization that both movements – that of the full and equal participation of women and that of the full and equal dignity and respect accorded to all religions – can only develop in a free, open and democratic society where traditional hierarchies and leadership based on ascription are no longer the norm. In this sense interreligious dialogue, however understood as itself a religious event of far-reaching influence, is a child of modern secular and post-colonial society.

From a historical point of view it is interesting to note that the major starting-point now remembered as the beginning of the contemporary 'dialogue' process, the 1893 World's Parliament of Religions, was conceived within the context of the colonial setting of the 'Columbian Exposition' at Chicago. The considerable contribution of women to this World Fair has been researched in general terms,[8] but less is known about women's contribution to the World's Parliament of Religions. Rediscovering their voices in order to show how women participated in interreligious dialogue within a secular context right from the inception of this process is an important task of historical recovery in the history of the interfaith movement.[9] It is of special interest in this context that participants of this first parliament greatly highlighted the contribution and presence of women, much more than was the case for example at the centennial celebrations in 1993. One of the nineteen women plenary speakers at the 1893 event – the Revd Antoinette Brown Blackwell, the first Christian woman to be ordained, in 1853 – emphasized the need for more women to be active as preachers and pastors, for in her view the work of women was 'indispensable to the religious evolution of the human race'.[10]

From a greater contemporary awareness of women's contribution to the fields of religion and spirituality, and accepting the more refined theoretical gender perspectives of today, we can see how a very important point was being made here, but also how the historiography of an event again, as so often, has marginalized the presence and contribution of women. But I consider it worth emphasizing that the challenge of feminism for interreligious dialogue is a *spiritual* one, which may also develop into a *theological challenge* if feminist thinkers scrutinize the currently used categories in the theology of religions.

Much has been written on dialogue. The scholarly analysis and debate about the process of dialogue represents another form of *dialogue at a meta-level*, a reflective activity of theorizing which makes us stand back from the primary, experientially rooted activity of listening, speaking and sharing in dialogue, from the attempt to enter into an in-depth participation in a person's and a people's mode of thinking, believing, praying, meditating or worshipping. There exist different models of interreligious communication[11] which occur in different historical and social contexts, yet also somehow take place in spite of that context, involving relationship, trust and mutuality.

Several Christian theologians are now engaged in developing a new theology of religions and of interreligious dialogue. Their theoretical discussions make much use of the tripartite model of *exclusivism, inclusivism* and *pluralism*. The meaning and appropriateness of each of these terms have been much debated. There is no doubt that they have stimulated considerable critical reflection and advanced some of our understanding. I am not concerned with the full theological dimensions of this debate here, but should nonetheless like to make some critical observations.

First, there is the general question of the nature of theological discourse and its relationship to life-worlds. Many people, not only women, find theological language rather logocentric and remote, not to say 'lifeless', and rather inclined to what has been aptly described as 'violence of abstraction'. These three categories of exclusivism, inclusivism and pluralism appear much too narrow, static and insufficiently differentiated to capture the organic, fluid and dynamic reality of religion at a personal and social level. Nor do they in any way allude to the subtleties and existential commitment of faith. But someone might object that this is not their main task, which, on the contrary, consists in bearing on the analysis of the kinds of relationships that pertain between different religions. Yet for this important aim they are rather lacking in subtle nuance, so necessary to capture dynamic complexity.

Secondly, from the perspective of women they are also thoroughly androcentric in the sense that they are presented as universally applicable and comprehensive categories for dealing with the relationships between different religions without taking the specific conditions of people into account. This means that the variable of gender is neither implicitly nor explicitly taken note of, so that one can justifiably raise the question whether women of faith can relate their own experience to these abstractions or whether other, more relational categories are required to account for the activity and experience of interreligious dialogue in a more integral and comprehensive manner.

In the context of discussing the theological challenges posed by the existence of religious pluralism and by the development of greater contact and dialogue between people of different faiths it is imperative to reckon with the global, cross-cultural dialogue occurring among women worldwide today. But this critical, feminist dialogue of women challenges or potentially even subverts interreligious dialogue as it is conducted at present.

Women are coming into their own in the field of religious pluralism by critiquing the patriarchal and sexist nature of religions while at the same time examining much more closely the feminine dimension of religious symbolism and the actual role of women in religion. So often women are considered as subordinate, as less than fully human, as marginal in different religious teachings, and mostly they are not given access to positions of leadership and authority. Thus one must ask searching questions: Is the interreligious dialogue, as currently conducted, really relevant to women? How much of its language, representation and activity is exclusive rather than truly inclusive?

Ten years ago, when I was invited to give the Cardinal Heenan Lecture on Christian ecumenism,[12] I asked: 'Where are the women in ecumenism? What is women's own dialogue about? What can women's experience of dialogue contribute to a new vision of ecumenism?' The same questions can be asked with regard to women's potential in making a full and equal contribution to the dialogue of religions. This opens up a whole new field of enquiry and allows for the development of new horizons in the encounter of religions. But much work needs to be done before this will really happen, for at present much of interreligious dialogue is not all that relevant to women; much of it is hurtful and exclusive; and much of it takes no account at all of current developments in either women's spirituality or women's critical work on religion. Nor are the dialoguing men aware of the new dialogue among women today.

Contemporary feminism presents a considerable challenge for inter-religious dialogue, although at present this challenge has not been fully articulated. But one can also look at this unequal relation the other way round and ask: What is the challenge of interreligious dialogue for feminist women?

The challenge of interreligious dialogue for feminism

Secular feminism debates racial and cultural, but never religious, pluralism. Feminist theologians, on the other hand, have been primarily concerned with a critical resifting of the Jewish and Christian religious traditions rather than with the encounter and relations between different religions. A few works, such as Maureen O'Neill's *Women Speaking, Women Listening*,[13] have looked at women's involvement with interreligious dialogue, but there has been little of a feminist reception or critique of the interfaith movement and theological debate about dialogue so far.[14] This is also evident from the World Council of Churches 1995 publication on *Women's Visions*[15] which celebrates the theological work undertaken by women during the Decade of Churches in Solidarity with Women. While the reports in this publication point to the search for a new paradigm of women and men in relationship reshaping humankind, ecclesiology, theology, morality and a new anthropology together,[16] the women's debate is carried on entirely within the Christian universe of discourse, yet without explicitly reflecting on the new theological developments linked to interreligious dialogue among Christians themselves.

As these reports are based on Christian feminist theological developments around the world, this book is a good example which shows clearly that feminist theology, though wide-ranging and internally very diverse itself, is not yet critically wrestling with the challenge of religious pluralism and its implications for theology and spirituality at a theoretical and practical level. Nor has it examined the prevailing concepts and language of the theology of religions from a feminist perspective.

Yet the existence and lively debate of interreligious dialogue challenge some of the limitations of feminist theology itself and invite it to widen its horizons and draw on theological and spiritual resources from different religious traditions. Among feminist theologians it is particularly those from the non-Western world, especially from Asia, who are more open to reflect on the challenge of religious pluralism. Religious diversity is more acknowledged but not necessarily theoretically more fully reflected upon, as can be seen in the readings found in my anthology *Feminist Theology from the Third World*.[17]

Given the great wisdom traditions of Asia, and the numerically small presence of Christians on the Asian continent, it comes as no surprise that Asian religious feminists organized a women's interfaith meeting for Buddhist, Christian, Hindu, Jewish and Muslim women as well as those from indigenous traditions in Kuala Lumpur, in 1989. In their Report *Faith Renewed*[18] they stressed as their objectives, among others, the 'deepening of one's own and other faiths, from a woman's perspective' and 'fostering mutuality, respect, solidarity and sisterhood by overcoming divisive barriers'. In each case the women examined both the liberative and oppressive aspects of their respective religions and looked at the practical, social, legal and economic effects of the religious and socio-cultural discrimination against women. Their vision was to reclaim the positive values for women in their respective cultures and religions, but also 'to conscientise women and men' about their objectives.[19]

This is one example of women themselves becoming actively engaged in interreligious dialogue, although these women did not reflect on current international discussions on dialogue among men or critique it. Yet it is especially in Asia, so much at the crossroads of the encounter of cultures and religions, that we find a particularly challenging and fertile environment for the mutual impact of feminism and interfaith encounter. In this context it is interesting to note that the German feminist theologian Elisabeth Gössmann, who knows Asia well through her many years' teaching in Japan, has included a whole section on feminism and interreligious dialogue in her wide-ranging article on the 'Feminist critique of universal claims to truth',[20] wherein she highlights the thoroughly androcentric character of traditional Christian theology which is an all-male theology – and that applies also to the theology of religions.

Thus the process of dialogue is still very gender-specific and restricted. Whereas men's interreligious dialogue does not appropriate the insights of women's dialogue, women's interreligious dialogue, where it exists, does not yet critically analyse and call into question the androcentrism and exclusiveness of male dialogue. These two different forms of dialogue challenge each other.

The challenge of women's dialogue to structures and institutions concerned with interreligious dialogue

Today feminist writers on religion are critiquing the patriarchal framework of all the religions of the world. They are recovering women's own voices and contributions, their religious roles and rituals, feminine images and metaphors used for constructs of Ultimate Reality, and women's heritage in spirituality and mysticism. The feminist critique of religion has been furthest advanced in Christianity and Judaism, but women from other religions – whether Hinduism, Buddhism, Islam, Sikhism, Chinese, Japanese or African religions, or other native religious traditions – are now applying feminist analyses to their respective faiths. Thus women are working on the transformation of world religions from within their own traditions by critiquing the androcentric and patriarchal framework of their scriptural and doctrinal heritage, and by recovering muted female voices and experiences from the past. This is an immense task of recovery and reconstruction, but at the same time there exists also the great challenge of constructing new forms of thought and new institutional structures which are more flexible and empowering than those of the past and which can help to transform patriarchal religions.

If the development of interreligious dialogue is a challenge for all religions today, a challenge for education, theology and spirituality, this dialogue itself is challenged by the crying need of global movements searching for justice, peace, ecological balance, and the liberation of all oppressed people, many of whom are women. More than a decade ago the Sri Lankan Jesuit Aloysius Pieris, in his 'religiously motivated desire and decision to move toward the new humanity', reflected on 'The place of non-Christian religions and cultures in the evolution of Third World theology',[21] where he underlined the need for a theology of religions that will expand the existing boundaries of orthodoxy by entering 'into the liberative streams of other religions and cultures'. One wonders how far this is really happening. Without explicitly engaging with the feminist perspective, Pieris's article contains the brief statement: 'Sexism points to an uncivilized area in religion. The new cosmological order that the Third World clamors for includes unhampered feminine participation in religion and revolution.'[22]

This is a truly provocative statement. If sexism represents an as yet *uncivilized* area of religion, a not yet fully 'hominized' development as Teilhard de Chardin would have called it, then we shall have to work for the further full development of religion as an integral part of a fully developed humanity. Pieris's statement also points to the profound truth that religious, social, political and economic transformations are interlinked and cannot achieve an overall impact without the full and equal participation of women.

Although the contemporary interfaith movement has produced the Chicago 'Declaration toward a global ethic',[23] there is at present little evidence that interreligious dialogue has influenced any concrete political or social developments. It is to be welcomed that this declaration entitles one of its four directives a 'Commitment to a culture of equal rights and partnership between men and women', but unfortunately this partnership is only discussed in terms of sexual and familial relations. When it is said that 'all over the world there are condemnable forms of patriarchy, domination of one sex over the other, exploitation of women, sexual misuse of children, and forced prostitution', why is no connection made with the patriarchal exploitation and subordination of women by the religions themselves? The directive is phrased as if the religions already had the answer to the oppression and exploitation of women, whereas religions themselves are part of the problem and cause of this oppressive state of affairs.

A far more perceptive and detailed analysis is needed, enquiring into the religious norms and practices affecting the dynamics of gender construction, the formation of subject and gender identity, in order to make clear how religions themselves are oppressive to women. This is particularly true with regard to the centuries-old negative evaluation of women's sexuality which has caused and legitimized oppressive structures for women in all religions, as a comparative WCC study has shown.[24]

In the past, religions often defined themselves in isolation, apart from each other, whereas now they have to interpret their teachings and practices in an interreligious and intercultural context in relation to each other. This introduces a new element of complexity which requires a broadening of the field of enquiry. Given our current debates, it also demands serious attention to gender issues as they affect women and men. But at present this is not happening in the interfaith debate.

I have tried to argue that both interreligious dialogue and religious feminism could gain from giving space and attention to the dialogue of the other. Judith G. Martin speaks of the need for the 'en-gendering' of dialogue and the enrichment which would result out of the convergence of dialogue among religious 'dialogians' and feminists.[25] She writes:

> Despite the existence of dialogical paradigms which provide various
> frameworks for affirming religious pluralism, interfaith dialogue
> remains handicapped and weakened by the ongoing discrimination
> and unequal treatment of women and minorities by the faith

communities engaged in dialogue. Sexism inhibits bonding and thus interferes with dialogue within and across traditions.[26]

It is evident that interreligious dialogue remains part of patriarchy. To envision and develop a post-patriarchal dialogue it will be necessary to do away with all exclusions and hierarchies, especially the hierarchy of gender which is so pervasive in religions. Radical institutional and doctrinal transformations are needed to respond to the need of women for equal participation and dignity, and the demand to condemn all prejudice and violence against women, especially those done in the name of religion. We still have a long way to go before we reach that goal, but in recognition of this important aim two Christian women organized a group of about a dozen women from different faiths (Buddhism, Christianity, Hinduism, Islam, Sikhism, Zoroastrianism) to formulate a resolution submitted to the Parliament of the World's Religions in 1993 – unfortunately never debated, though signed by most of the main speakers and different religious representatives – to declare 1993–2003 a 'Decade of Religions in Solidarity with Women'.

I think such a new decade, worked for and helped by all those engaged in interreligious dialogue, would be a tremendous challenge. At present there is still much work and change needed before religions will accord equal space and full justice to women. Women's great invisibility, marginality and voicelessness in world religions are paralleled by the marginality and voicelessness of women in inter-religious dialogue. If more women became more prominent and visible in such dialogue, this in turn might help to transform the oppressive patriarchal structures of religions and produce more compelling, more just and inclusive, but also more gender-aware religious worlds which would be more life-sustaining and life-enhancing for all peoples and the earth.

Contemporary feminism has a bearing on interpreting religious scriptures, on reforming religious practices and structures, on religious education, on questions of justice and peace and on the understanding of spirituality – in fact on all the questions considered under the topic *Pluralism and the Religions*. Contemporary critical feminism contains, both explicitly and implicitly, strong social and political dimensions. Women's demand to be listened to, to be fully acknowledged and included on equal terms is itself a political act. At present, feminism remains a missing dimension in interreligious dialogue. If it were to become a truly integral part, this would mean a radical political and theological transformation of all interreligious relations as presently conceived. It might also mean a new birth and fuller disclosure of the powers of the Spirit whose oneness embraces and transcends all differences, as many religions so frequently preach and proclaim, but much less often translate into practice.

Notes

1 In John Stratton Hawley (ed.), *Fundamentalism and Gender* (New York and Oxford: Oxford University Press, 1994), pp. 175–201.

2 In Hawley, *Fundamentalism and Gender*, p. 199.

3 Wilfred Cantwell Smith, *Towards a World Theology: Faith and the Comparative History of Religion* (London: Macmillan, 1981), p. 43 (repr. New York, 1989).

4 Marcus Braybrooke, *Inter-Faith Organizations 1893–1979: An Historical Directory* (New York and Toronto: The Edwin Mellen Press, 1980).

5 Francis Clark, *Interfaith Directory* (New York: International Religious Foundation, 1987).

6 Celia and David Storey (eds), *Visions of an Interfaith Future: Proceedings Sarva–Dharma–Sammelana, Religious People Meeting Together, Bangalore, India, 19–22 August 1993* (Oxford: International Interfaith Centre, 1994). It is worth noting that women's spirituality is discussed by a Korean Won Buddhist nun in that volume, but she does not reflect on the wider implications of this perspective for interfaith dialogue: Rev. Chung Ok Lee, 'Women's spirituality: Won Buddhism perspective', ibid., pp. 124–7.

7 See Marcus Braybrooke, *Faith in a Global Age: The Interfaith Movement's Offer of Hope to a World in Agony: A Personal Perspective* (Oxford: Braybrooke Press, 1995), p. 2, where the author states that he began to speak of the 'interfaith movement' from 1978 onwards so as to suggest that participants were not rivals but part of something bigger. See also his larger historical study – *Pilgrimage of Hope: One Hundred Years of Global Interfaith Dialogue* (London: SCM, 1992). Neither this detailed history nor the monograph of personal reflections includes any awareness of gender differences and concerns.

8 See Jeanne Madeline Weimann, *The Fair Women: The Story of The Woman's Building, World's Columbian Exposition, Chicago 1893* (Chicago: Academy Chicago, 1981).

9 This point has not been specifically noted in Marcus Braybrooke's history *Pilgrimage of Hope* (see note 7). I have examined the contributions of women plenary speakers at the 1893 World's Parliament of Religions in my article 'Rediscovering women's voices at the World's Parliament of Religions' in E. J. Ziolkowski (ed.), *A Museum of Faiths: Histories and Legacies of the 1893 World's Parliament of Religions* (Classics in Religious Studies; Atlanta, GA: Scholars Press and American Academy of Religion, 1993), pp. 325–43.

10 King, 'Rediscovering women's voices', p. 334.

11 See Ursula King, 'Models of interreligious communications: reflections on interfaith dialogue' in D. Cohn-Sherbok (ed.), *Many Mansions: Inter-*

faith and Religious Intolerance (London: Bellew Publishing, 1992), pp. 107–221.

12 See Ursula King, 'Women in dialogue: a new vision of ecumenism', *Heythrop Journal* XVI (1985), pp. 125–42.

13 (Maryknoll, NY: Orbis Books, 1990); see also Diana L. Eck and Devaki Jain (eds), *Speaking of Faith: Cross-cultural Perspectives on Women, Religion and Social Change* (New Delhi: Kali for Women, and London: The Women's Press, 1986); Virginia Ramey Mollenkott (ed.), *Women of Faith in Dialogue* (New York: Crossroad, 1988). For a critical discussion of the connections between justice, religious pluralism and a feminist perspective which 'must radically affirm religious pluralism', see Marjorie Hewitt Suchoki, 'In search of justice' in John Hick and Paul F. Knitter (eds), *The Myth of Christian Uniqueness: Toward a Pluralistic Theology of Religions* (Maryknoll, NY: Orbis Books, 1989), pp. 149–61.

14 Since my original writing of this chapter, Kate McCarthy has published her article 'Women's experience as a hermeneutical key to a Christian theology of religions', *Studies in Interreligious Dialogue* 6/2 (1996), pp. 163–73. She argues that women's experience – rooted in a new kind of affirmation of religious difference, a life lived at the margins, and an embodied spirituality – can enrich a Christian theology of pluralism in the area of hermeneutics and provide a more fluid conception of God and a different understanding of Christology. This is substantiated by drawing very selectively on the work of several women theologians (Carter Heyward of the United States, Ivone Gebara of Brazil, Mercy Oduyoye of Ghana and Chung Hyun Kyung from Korea). The article makes the important point that Christian feminist theology offers resources for a new approach to a Christian theology of religions, but it does not explicitly analyse the androcentric and exclusive character of this theology nor does it engage with the work of the few other feminist writers on religious pluralism (see notes 12, 13 and 20).

15 Ofelia Ortega (ed.), *Women's Visions: Theological Reflection, Celebration, Action* (Geneva: WCC, 1995).

16 Ibid., p. 75.

17 Ursula King (ed.), *Feminist Theology from the Third World* (London: SPCK, and Maryknoll, NY: Orbis Books, 1994).

18 Dulcie Abraham, Sun Ai Lee Park and Yvonne Dahlin (eds), *Faith Renewed: A Report on the First Asian Women's Consultation on Interfaith Dialogue* (Hong Kong: Asian Women's Resource Centre for Culture and Theology, 1989).

19 Abraham et al., *Faith Renewed*, pp. 117, 119. See also Mukti Barton, 'Scripture as empowerment for liberation and justice: the experience of Christian and Muslim women in Bangladesh', PhD dissertation, University of Bristol (1998).

20 Elisabeth Gössmann, 'Feministische Kritik an universalen Wahrheitsansprüchen' in Anton Peter (ed.), *Christlicher Glaube in multireligiöser Gesellschaft: Erfahrungen, theologische Reflexionen, missionarische Per-*

spektiven (Immensee: Neue Zeitschrift für Missionswissenschaft, 1996), pp. 312-50; see especially the section 'Der interreligiöse Dialog und die Pluralität der weiblichen Standpunkte', pp. 340-7. Gössmann refers to the 'ultra-academic' and much too 'other-worldly' orientation of inter-religious dialogue and pleads for a shift in emphasis which will bring both genders more closely together in their efforts of dialoguing (see p. 350).

21 Aloysius Pieris, 'The place of non-Christian religions and cultures in the evolution of Third World theology' in Virginia Fabella and Sergio Torres (eds), *Irruption of the Third World: Challenge to Theology* (Maryknoll, NY: Orbis Books, 1983), pp. 113–39.

22 Pieris, ibid., p. 136. Since writing this chapter in 1983, Pieris has much more explicitly engaged with the feminist perspective which he considers 'a permanent feature in the struggle for full humanity'; see his important article 'Woman and religion in Asia: towards a Buddhist and Christian appropriation of the feminist critique', *Dialogue*, New Series, XIX–XX (1992–93), pp. 119–203, which is particularly significant for the under-standing of spirituality but does not explicitly consider the issues of feminism and interreligious dialogue discussed by me here.

23 See Hans Küng and Karl-Josef Kuschel, *A Global Ethic: The Declaration of the Parliament of the World's Religions* (London: SCM Press, 1993).

24 See Jeanne Becher (ed.), *Women, Religion and Sexuality: Studies on the Impact of Religious Teachings on Women* (Geneva: WCC, 1990).

25 Judith G. Martin, 'En-gendering the dialogue: feminist contributions to interfaith encounters', unpublished paper (New Delhi, February 1993).

26 Martin, ibid., p. 5.

Part Two

Pluralism and responsibility:
the political dimension

4

Theological education for pluralism in India

J. Rosario Narchison

1 The Indian scene

The choice of India for a case study in appropriate theological education is quite understandable. A home of many ancient religions and a land of countless other diversities, India stands in dire need of an education that would, first of all, help her people overcome the tensions and conflicts that keep on erupting, often in violent forms, from the competing interests of her various religious, ethnic, linguistic and caste communities. Secondly, and much more importantly, India needs a theological education that would bring to the fore all the potential the various religions of her people have for improving the quality of their life. In other words, we need in India a theological education of a different kind – one that is in the context of and at the service of the pluralism that deeply pervades our daily life. This education for pluralism is precisely what the school of theology that I represent at this conference is aiming at.

Inaugurated in November 1988, the Indian School of Ecumenical Theology (ISET) at Bangalore, India, has been pursuing a methodology which, in contrast to traditional Christian theology, helps the students so to understand their own religious traditions as to affirm and celebrate the significance of other religions and theologies. For ISET ecumenism means pluralism. Not a pluralism which in the name of universalism obliterates in subtle ways the innate and indigenous religious identities of other peoples. Not a pluralism which promotes the dominance of one religion's world-view over those of others. Not the *ecumenism of dominance* which was unfortunately put forward by the Central Committee of the World Council of Churches in 1951 by defining the 'ecumenical' as 'everything that relates to the whole task of the whole church to bring the Gospel to the whole world'. The dominance aspect of the above definition is unwittingly reinforced by a subsequent comment by John Makay that by this definition 'the Ecumenical Movement means both the missionary movement of the Church *to occupy the oikoumene* in the name of Christ and the ecclesiastical movement to unify the *forces of occupation*'.[1]

On the contrary the focus at the ISET, as we shall see, is on an *ecumenism of solidarity* among people of different faiths, solidarity not in spite of but because of differences.

The global context of religious communities in conflict has given rise to organizations such as the World Conference of Religions for Peace, World Congress of Faiths, International Association for Religious Freedom, and the like. But how much of actual education for pluralism these organizations, most of them financed by Christian agencies in the West, have been able to undertake, especially among communities of other faiths, is a rather delicate question. Such organizations often do not reach out to the people in actual conflict nor to persons working at grass-roots level in the Indian villages. ISET on its part, however, is actively engaged in offering such education for pluralism to specific target groups such as youth leaders, college teachers, Christian pastors, and teachers in theological colleges and seminaries. These groups, as we shall see, often include persons of other faiths such as Hindus, Muslims and Sikhs.

There are several compelling reasons why ISET has embarked on this experiment. The negative, and for some the most potent, reason is that religions in India are fast becoming forces for evil. In his 1973 book *The Temptations of Religion* Charles Davis had listed four temptations to which promoters of all religions are prone. They are, in his words, lust for certitude, cosmic vanity, pride of history and anger of morality.[2] In view of what is currently happening at the political level in India and elsewhere Davis would probably have highlighted another, more dangerous, temptation – namely, the political use or abuse of religion. It is seen in all its ugly manifestations all over India – from the never-ending Kashmir- and Punjab-related terrorism in the north to the sporadic Hindu–Muslim, Hindu–Christian conflicts in the south.

Religions make up the breeding-ground for what is known as 'communalism' in India and the Indian subcontinent. Bipan Chandra, an incisive analyst of the phenomenon, points to three stages in the growth of this communal ideology and the communal riots that ensue from it. First, a feeling is promoted that people of the same religion have not only *common* religious beliefs, but also *common* economic, political and cultural interests. This gives rise to religion-based communities all over India. In the second stage it is emphasized that the political, economic and social interests of one religious community are *different* from those of other religious communities. The third stage does not take long to emerge when people of one religious community are made to believe that their interests are not only different but also *antagonistic* to those of other communities.[3] Theological education for pluralism is precisely to combat the evil of communalism which in countries like India not only breeds aimless terrorism but also impedes the overall development of the people.

Positive reasons for the kind of theological education ISET is engaged in may be considered at two levels: at the level of theology and at that of human life.

At the level of theology, no theological education in India is meaningful without constant cross-reference to the diverse religions by which the people of India live. Education by mere self-reference which bases itself exclusively on one's own religious traditions may still be possible and permissible in the West, but not in India where the vast majority of the people continue to draw moral strength from religions other than Christian. Let it be emphasized here that despite several centuries of Western dominance Christians account for only 2.7 per cent of the population and the remaining 97.3 per cent are not animists or atheists but men and women guided by highly developed religious traditions and ethical principles.

To our utter shame, therefore, we realize today how theologically arrogant the world Christians were in repeating at Tambaram (near Madras) on the Indian soil, on the occasion of the general assembly of the International Missionary Council (IMC) in 1938, the theology of absolute discontinuity between biblical Christianity and other religions as advocated by Karl Barth for whom to dialogue with other religions was to howl with wolves ('heulen mit den Wölfen').[4] The star speaker at Tambaram, Hendrik Kraemer, continued to hold on to Barth's view that religion was a fundamental 'being in error' and in the light of Jesus Christ a humiliating aberration.[5]

The sad irony of it all was that the plea at that moment of a determined band of lay Indian Christian theologians at Madras, one of them P. Chenchiah, for recognizing the salvific value of the great religions of India did not merit even a footnote to the records of the said IMC assembly.[6] Now that with the dismantling of the colonial system Western dominance in the understanding of Christian faith is being gradually reduced, theological education for co-operation with adherents of other religions in our own country has become not only a possibility but also, as we shall see in the last part of this paper, a *political necessity* urging the people of all religions to make a decisive educational contribution to an authentic secularization of the educated and uneducated masses of India.

At the level of human life, the present rediscovery especially in the

Third World countries of the this-worldly (secular) concerns of the 'Jesus before Christianity' and the way he preferred the human to the religious calls for a new direction in theological education in India. No education will be relevant if it misses the two most striking features of the Indian reality: deep religiosity and miserable poverty, both of them often coexisting in the same people of the land. A major goal of theological education in India ought to be to enlist the co-operation of people of all religions to alleviate the evils of material poverty which is basically a spiritual problem stemming from an exploitative culture.[7] Theological education for pluralism is therefore premised on the conviction that the hope for a better India lies not in the inflow of more foreign capital but in the available resources of the people themselves, especially the liberative forces of their respective religions; not religion in general, but the diversity of religions by which the people of India live.

Wishing to speak more from my experience as a theological educator than from books, I have chosen to turn certain parts of this presentation into a kind of report on the working of the ISET whose first dean I happened to be, for six years (till April 1995). The paper is in three parts: first, the present general introduction to the Indian scene; second, by way of further input, a quick look at two uncommon aspects of ISET's methodology; and finally a few reflections on how theological education for pluralism is a political task required of all religions in India.

2 With all – from below

In the Bible God's word is addressed to particular contexts. Theology too should speak to the prevailing contexts. If theology is essentially reflection on the life-related implications of the God-encounter which is available to all human beings,[8] then the local languages and the people's culture, the problems and the possibilities of the different contexts in which people live ought to enter deeply into the texture of theological education. This, I believe, is a primary message of the 'incarnation' which still remains the central truth about the Christian religion. One therefore wonders why so basic a truth as this was ignored till recently in the project of Christian theological education in the Third World countries – why, for example, theological education in Roman Catholic institutions in India as a whole was imparted in the language of the élite of medieval Europe and why both Catholic and Protestant institutions by and large merely repeated in India the themes of Western theology such as One God, triune God, Christology (mostly the divinity of Christ), ecclesiology, sacramentology and the like, while Indian realities like poverty, political processes and plurality of faiths rarely became subjects for theological education.

The explanation, we need to confess humbly today, is to be found in what we may call the politics of Christian theological education, especially since the days of the colonial expansion of the West. To be brief, the primary aim of theological education was to support the cause of a certain *monoidentity* in religion. In other words, Christians were to be so theologically educated in exclusive (often denominational) groups as to be equipped for the task of reducing all peoples of India to one (Christian) identity or to what we call here monoidentity.[9] Christianity was to supersede all other religions and cultures.

This was in sharp contrast to the educational culture of Indian religions, as is evident in the spiritual impact Indian religions have had, with no noticeable traces of colonial exploitation, on the peoples of Myanmar, Thailand, Laos, Vietnam, Cambodia, Indonesia, China and Japan. Moreover, there are innumerable persons in India even today who would declare themselves as Hindus, Jains, Buddhists, Sikhs and Christians all at once. They see no incongruence in being so because for them names of religions (given by Europeans!) do not matter. Indians for millennia have been quite comfortable with composite cultures and even *composite religions*. To this feature of Indian religiosity we shall appeal in the last part of our presentation.

In the wake of Vatican II (1962–65) and of the WCC Assembly at New Delhi (1961) India stood in need of a new method in theology, and ISET had a double advantage which enabled it to respond appropriately. Bound neither to one church nor to any one particular foreign funding agency,[10] it has been free to experiment with a startlingly unconventional method. I limit myself to describing briefly only two aspects of this method with a view to clarifying further the meaning of 'Theological education for pluralism'.

1. Exclusive theological education for Christians alone does not make much sense in India today. Theology then would become another divisive factor in the already divided India. The theological courses offered at ISET, therefore, are so Christian that they are never meant for Christians alone! It is a common sight there to see Hindus, Muslims, Christians, Sikhs and 'unbelievers' all learning theology together. It often happens that the one-month course in ecumenical theology for Christian 'Pastors', for example, includes also Hindu and Muslim seekers and activists. Another important feature to be noted is that not only the learners but also the teachers or the resource persons are drawn from among adherents of all religions and no religion.

Those belonging to other faiths are never called non-Christians but always friends or neighbours of other faiths. In this respect ISET carries forward the spirit of its founder, the late M. A. Thomas, who in 1974 began his lecture to a group of Christians in New Jersey by asking the audience whether he could address them as 'dear non-Hindus of the United States'.[11] Do not the Hindus have a right to their own identity? Why then give them a Christian-centred label?

The experiment in 'mixed' theological education has taught us a couple of invaluable truths.

The first truth is that no effective communication in a context of religious pluralism is possible without a new language which modifies, if not totally abandons, the idioms and jargons inherited from an age of religious conflicts in the West. We realize, for example, that there is no need to invoke the name of Jesus Christ whenever we speak of God and humankind (theology). In this regard ISET still preserves the pre-Indian Independence spirit of Christian leaders in India like C. F. Andrews who, while supporting Mahatma Gandhi against British rule, declared: 'Christ has become not less central but more central and universal, not less divine to me but more so because more universally human.'[12]

Moreover, we Christians in India are one in spirit with our fellow countrymen of different faiths and, despite a long period of Western dominance in our theology and worship, we are still able to understand and speak the religious language of the Hindus and others. The *Mahabharata* and *Ramayana*, for example, are part of our common culture, and many Christians know these 'Hindu' epics much better than the Old or New Testaments! Theological education for pluralism at ISET provides the students with a new set of non-sectarian terms and concepts so that they may be able to enter into the spirit of religions other than their own.

Furthermore, by learning theology together persons of different faiths come face to face with the *mystery of many religions*. For us Indians religions are not mere historical accidents. To quote P. Chenchiah, one of the dissenting lay theologians at the 1938 Tambaram IMC conference to which we referred above,

> The Indian Christian never understands Jesus until he understands the drama of God's dealings with man in and through other religions of the world ... To us in India inter-relations of religions have become a matter of life and death. We can have no peace here or hereafter and *our nation can have no future* until we find the key to this mystery [of several religions in India].[13]

The second truth we learn from mixed theological education is that it is possible for people of different faiths to pray together. They not only pray together, but Hindus, Muslims, Sikhs and Christians also take turns in preparing and conducting common worship at ISET. Readings are taken from the Dhammapada, the Upanishads, the Koran and the Adi Granth along with those from the Bible. With the Psalms are sung the soul-stirring poems of Rabindranath Tagore. One of the assignments for the students at the end of the course for pastors reads: 'As an Indian Christian I consider my Bible larger than that of Western Christians; it includes the *Gita*, the *Koran* and *Dhammapada* – offer your comment on the above statement.'

Such mixed education and worship reveal to the learners the genuine devotion of others. An incident in the life of the founder is worth recalling here. As a college student with some evangelistic fervour, he reports, he once went to a senior lecturer of his and, with a view to 'converting' him, described to him how Jesus was a living reality in his life. The lecturer replied: 'Yes, Mr Thomas, I can understand it, because Lord Krishna is a living reality to me.'[14] In this context it is not without significance that in the campus of the Ecumenical Christian Centre, whose programme ISET is, no single 'conversion' to Christianity has taken place during the 32 years of its existence and that the majority of its employees are practising Hindus.

Evangelicals, including D. L. Moody's disciple John R. Mott, who were determined to 'conquer the world for Christ', were the first ecumenists. Evangelicals, after all, invented the ecumenical movement, declares Richard Lovelace. But here is a school of *ecumenical* theology which teaches students to understand and appreciate other religions! 'Ecumenical' and 'evangelical' seem to have become antonyms. And that, in the opinion of Michael Kinnamon, 'is enough to set earlier generations of Protestants rolling in their graves'.[15]

2. Another uncommon aspect of ISET's methodology is that almost every programme in theological education begins from below, from the concrete world. The motivating force, of course, is faith in God and the future of humankind. But it is a faith that does not dabble in abstract and abstruse concepts, but comes to grips with God's world in action. It is a faith that looks upon the 'missionary' mandate of Jesus as an ongoing task – not for numerical conversions but for creating a new social awareness, for a new culture which is not exploitative, and for bringing forth the *Übermensch*, a nobler kind of human being (not exactly the kind Nietzsche had in mind).

Theological education for pluralism, we believe, cannot be content with what Paulo Freire calls *alphabetization*, a nutritionist approach of adding new concepts to old theology, but must start with what he calls *problematization*,[16] an acute awareness of the problems and blessings of life in a pluralistic world.

To illustrate our point, let me refer to ISET's annual month-long theological programme for youth leaders, which after a quick look at the Indian meaning of ecumenism enters into an in-depth exposure of the students to the ground reality of India in these words:

Situation
  a   economic, political, social, cultural and religious
  b   oppression, structures of injustice and poverty
  c   forces for the status quo, fundamentalism, caste, illiteracy, dominant culture . . . [17]

This methodology, much more than the traditional one, places theological education in Third World countries at the service of social change. It is as much concerned about relevance as about identity which unfortunately was almost an obsession with the old heresy-conscious theology. It allows ample space for theological reflection, besides God, on such vulnerable segments of humanity as the women, the poor, the unemployed, the dalits, the landless labourers and the like. It constantly reminds the students that it is in the real-life struggles and hopes of the peoples that God-encounter primarily takes place. The 'experience' of God in prayer and worship, in scripture reading and contemplation, can only be of secondary importance.[18]

In one sense, all our past efforts through theological education to impose one religion on the whole world were in wilful ignorance of God's ways. To begin theological education with a knowledge of this pluralistic world is to be forewarned of an elementary truth about all reality, as articulated by Thomas Berry:

This law of diversity holds not only for the other areas of being and of action but also for the religious life of the human community, for revelation, belief, spiritual disciplines, and sacramental forms. If there is revelation, it will not be singular but differentiated. If there is grace it will be differentiated in its expression. If there are spiritual disciplines or sacraments or sacred communities they will be differentiated. The greater the differentiation, the greater the perfection of the whole since perfection is in the interacting diversity; the extent of the diversity is the measure of the perfection.[19]

In making the actual world the *point de départ* of theological education ISET gives expression to a basic conviction of its founder. When asked at the very evening of his 80-year-long life if he still believed that there was no salvation outside the church he replied that he had once held that position and that now he tended to believe that 'outside the world there is no salvation'![20]

3 *Theological education – a political task*

Now we come to the core content of the theological education for pluralism attempted at the ISET. In one sentence, while it is quite legitimate and necessary for conventional institutions to clarify through theological education the implications of God-encounter for life (the elementary definition we have given above of 'theology'), ISET on its part aims at training leaders who would assist at an authentic secularization of the Indian masses whose religiosity in the political situation presently prevailing in India is a serious obstacle to their own individual and collective survival, let alone advancement.

Secularism as an ideology and secularization as a social process have been the *bête noire* of Western Christianity. In reality, however, they were born of the heart-rending struggle of Western men and women for freedom from the unitary and oppressive ideology of the church(es). Secularization for many meant the will to breathe the air of freedom, to grow in a context of pluralism, to make room for views other than those of the churches/religions. Pluralism and secularism are two sides of the same coin; education for pluralism means education for secularism.

Secularism in the West developed for long in spite of Christianity. For a country like India, first of all, the distinction between the secular and the sacred in public life did not make much sense till modern notions crept in. All her indigenous religious traditions are secular in the twin sense of acceptance of many ways (to God) and many cultures, and concern for this world (*saeculum*) in all aspects of its life. Texts to this effect in Hindu–Buddhist–Jain scriptures are too many to be selectively quoted here. Let me, however, point to one important fact about ancient Indian religiosity: the four ideals (*purusharthas*) after which human beings ought to strive are: *artha, dharma, kama* and *moksha*, and you notice that pursuit of wealth (*artha*) and enjoyment of life (*kama*) occupy a prominent place among them.[21] No *dharma* (religion)[22] to the exclusion of *artha* and *kama*! Secondly, coming to the day-to-day life of the Indian people, on the pluralistic front it is said that every Indian knows more than one language and every neighbourhood in India resounds with a host of languages. Into the same Indian family are born children of varied complexions and physiognomies – black, white and brown, the so-called Dravidian, Aryan and Mongoloid. Persons of different faiths marry into the same family and the church laws concerning *paritas cultus* (parity of cult) make sense only to Christians!

Now we understand why ISET from the very beginning interpreted ecumenism for India as secularism, and only very secondarily as church unity. This, I must admit, initially upsets those participants of our courses who come to learn about ways and means of uniting the churches. Incidentally, the encomium lavished on church unions in India such as the Church of South India and the Church of North India by the General Secretary of the WCC during his recently concluded visit to India (October 1995)[23] notwithstanding, we in India know from experience that unity of churches has been no guarantee for community of persons, and the so-called 'union' churches find themselves unable to be delivered from those problems of caste and wealth that plague society at large.[24]

Unity at the level of human needs and values is more essential to India today than mere, often irrelevant, church unity. We are happy that the indigenous scriptures and the way of life in India provide a strong secular basis for human unity. In fact, ISET offers a few sessions, usually by the noted Roman Catholic theologian Samuel Rayan, on the 'Hindu foundations of Christian ecumenism'. Here it is shown to the students how the Hindu (scriptural and life) traditions in general uphold mutual respect and tolerance amidst plurality of beliefs and perceptions, just as Jesus and the early church did. It is quite refreshing to note how in the matter of religious tolerance Jesus was and is more on the side of Hinduism than on that of Western Christianity of the Middle Ages! The secular vision of Jesus will be further enriched by the affirmation of the *maya* (illusory) nature of our fragmentary perception of God and reality, the primacy of *dharma* as praxis (not propositional faith), *ahimsa* (non-violence) in its negative and positive aspects and *shanti* as inner peace and harmony of the created order. These would constitute a valuable Hindu (Indian) contribution to the theology of ecumenism. The real threat to the secularity of the Indian people is from Western modernity. As K. C. Abraham, one of the frequently invited resource persons at the ISET, has recently pointed out, 'our (Indian) everyday life and relationships in the rural areas are plural. But, the reality of pluralism comes under severe test in the political realm which is governed by a monolithic state structure and rigid ideologies.'[25]

ISET, therefore, looks upon theological education for pluralism as a *political task* required of all religions in India. Hence, as we said above, here persons of different faiths learn theology together. In the West, secularism and secularization may still be suspect; but to the people of India, as Chenchiah declared in the statement quoted above,[26] there is no future except by way of pluralism which in concrete terms means secularism. A process of secularization with profound respect for life and the divine performs in India certain functions which no organized religion as such can render. We may mention three of them here.

First, out of a people of diverse faiths, races, castes and languages secularism alone can bring forth a *national political community* called State which would guarantee to all of them, irrespective of their religious and other differences, justice, liberty, equality and fraternity as promised in the preamble of the Indian Constitution. Thanks to secularism an ancient civilization can become a modern nation. Such secularism need not be an anti-religious dogma, as happened once with the West. It can very well be, as national leaders like Gandhi demonstrated in their lives, an *open secularism*, open to the influences of social ethics inspired by religious beliefs. Secularism is needed to make religion more tolerant and politics more moral.

Secondly, by loosening gradually through appropriate legislation the traditional bond between religion and culture, secularism can promote the quest for a *common religious culture* which would promote common social goals. For Christians, secularism makes another demand. As the meeting of the Directors of the Christian Institutes for the Study of Religion and Society in Asia at Nagpur in 1961 declared,

> the general loosening of the bond between culture and religion has had
> its effect on the Christian minorities in these Asian lands who have
> been enabled to begin to dissociate the Christian faith from Western
> culture and to identify themselves increasingly with the culture of their
> own countries.[27]

Secularism weakens the hold of religion on society, and by providing a much-needed critique of religion on behalf of man makes the state an instrument of modernization.

Thirdly, and most importantly in the context of political modernity, secularism guarantees the rights of minority communities in an ethnically, religiously and linguistically pluralistic nation like India. The division of the Indian people into majority and minority communities is an unfortunate fallout of the introduction of Western parliamentary democracy into India. What the media describe as *communal* violence in countries like Bangladesh, India (especially the regions of Kashmir and Punjab), Myanmar, Nepal, Pakistan and Sri Lanka has less to do with religion as such than with the scramble for money and power in a West-inspired democratic system. The Christian West has, in one sense, imported communalism into India. An Indian scholar reminds us that the term 'communalism' in a negative sense is used only in ex-British colonies.[28]

We need a theological education which would restore to religions their secular responsibilities. How does the ISET go about this task?

Besides the short-term seminars and workshops on communalism, fundamentalism, secularism and related topics (which usually are not yet part of the regular curricula of theological colleges and seminaries), ISET helps Hindus, Muslims, Christians and others realize, perhaps for the first time,

1   that the *history* of the so-called chosen people of the Old Testament
     is not the only history in which God has been at work and that
     every human group of every religion has a salvation history of its
     own;
2   that the *Christian Sacraments*, especially Baptism and Eucharist, are
     not symbols of exclusivism and communalism but expressions of
     commitment to break down the walls of separation among God's
     one human family;
3   and that the Bible of the Christians abounds in models of faith
     among adherents of other religions and that God is too great to be
     exhausted by the *Sacred Scriptures* of one religion alone. The sum-
     maries of courses offered by some eminent Indian theologians in
     this regard are reprinted in the official organ of the ISET.[29]

Serious misgivings have been voiced by some in recent times over the
likely perils and pitfalls involved in any uncritical promotion of religious pluralism. The Indian theologian Raimundo Panikkar is one of
them. A couple of years ago Paul F. Knitter in a theological forum at
Bangalore, India, summarized and critiqued Panikkar's views in this
regard.[30] Earlier in 1987, Tom F. Driver in a postscript to a volume on
religious pluralism[31] had elaborated empathetically on the arguments
of Kenneth Surin who had distanced himself from the team that
produced the above-mentioned volume. Both Knitter and Driver seem
to agree to some extent with Panikkar that a theological education for
pluralism, such as the one I outline here, may create more problems
than solve them. Among these are:

1   emergence of a facile and false universalism which would obliter-
     ate the identities of different faiths;
2   encouragement of a sense of self-complacency which by assuming
     a positive attitude towards other religions would overlook the need
     for each one's religion to be radically critiqued and reformed;
3   danger of compromising with such intolerable quasi-religious
     ideologies as the Nazism of recent memory and reactionary funda-
     mentalism of the *Hindutva* brand which is presently killing the
     secular soul of India; and
4   the spread of an ideological cover in the name of interfaith bon-
     homie over the 'disjunctions, disunities, distances and dissonances'
     that still pervade human society at the socio-economic-political
     level.[32]

From my own experience at the ISET I can attest, to some extent, to
the validity of these misgivings. Students hailing from *dalit* (lower
caste) backgrounds, for example, hesitate to take an interest in interfaith

dialogue for fear that it is a clever device of the upper-caste élite to reimpose brahminical language and themes on their own indigenous religious beliefs and practices. Many see in the Christian promotion of religious pluralism yet another plot to colonize people of other lands – this time at the level of religion – to the neglect of the more urgent problems of poverty and unemployment.

A more dangerous fallout of the kind of theological education for pluralism we attempt at the ISET is the likely reinforcement in the minds of the students of the age-old Indian attitude of indifference to authentic and inauthentic values in different religions. This attitude is often expressed in such statements as 'all religions lead to the same God just as all rivers flow into the same ocean'! They forget that many rivers do not reach the ocean and that religions have as much to do with human societies as with God. Thus at the political level secularism has degenerated into a passive role which in the name of 'equal respect' for all religions and for fear of offending the religious sensibilities of the people allows inhuman and intolerable practices to flourish. The state has ceased to be a critic of religion. Politicization of religion has become the order of the day. An unholy alliance has been created between politicians, criminals and godmen.[33]

Furthermore, theological education for pluralism in India may find it hard to overcome the newly released forces of communalism. The materialistic culture promoted by the present trend towards economic liberalization and subserved by the Western parliamentary system (where vote banks determine the future of India) drives each religion-based community to make its own demands. Until the time of Indian independence (1947) communalism was associated with the demands of religious minorities such as Muslims, Christians, Sikhs and Parsees. Today it is the *majority communalism* with its strident call for a Hindu *Rashtra* (nation) that is tearing apart the very fabric of Indian society.

If I have dwelt at some length on the challenges confronting theological education for pluralism it is because I believe that the task before us needs to be studied and discussed further. But more than study and discussion, *practical steps towards unity of faiths* are necessary.

The composite nature of Indian culture and religion, described above, confronts Christianity with a few practical questions. Will the Christian churches train and send their workers (ministers?) not to particular parishes or congregations, but to the human communities living in our villages and towns? Will Christian ministry in India focus its attention on building *base human communities* where religions are for men and women and not men and women for religions? Will the Christian churches encourage people of different faiths and ideologies to gather together, pray and plan together, using liberative texts from the various scriptures of our land, even going to the extent of alternately assembling together in a Hindu temple on one day, in a mosque on the next day, in a church the next day, and so on? Fear of the 'dangers' of pluralism mentioned above cannot stop us from building human communities in love and service.

The time has come for Christianity and all religions to review radically the purpose and method of theological education.

Notes

1 Emphases added. It is to be noted that a later spokesperson of the WCC has come down very hard on this definition. Cf. Ans J. Van der Bent, *God So Loves the World: The Immaturity of World Christianity* (Maryknoll, NY: Orbis Books, 1979), pp. 21–7; for Makay's comment, see his editorial in *Theology Today* 9 (April 1952), pp. 5–6.

2 Charles Davis, *The Temptations of Religion* (New York: Harper & Row, 1973).

3 Bipan Chandra, *Communalism in Modern India* (New Delhi: Vani Educational Books, 1984), pp. 1–4.

4 Quoted in Isaac Padinjarekuttu, *The Missionary Movement of the 19th and 20th Centuries and Its Encounter with India* (Frankfurt am Main: Peter Lang, 1995), p. 211, n. 65.

5 Quoted in Stanley J. Samartha, 'Mission in a religiously plural world: looking beyond Tambaram 1938', *International Review of Mission* 77 (1988), pp. 311–24 (p. 312).

6 For the Madras Rethinking Group, see their joint volume, G. V. Job et al., *Rethinking Christianity in India* (Madras: Hogarth Press, 1938).

7 Cf. J. Rosario Narchison, 'Exploitative culture systems and Christ' in Jacob Kavunkal and F. Hrangkhuma (eds), *Christ and Cultures* (Bombay: St Paul's, 1994), pp. 213–37; K. N. Panikkar, 'Globalisation and culture', *The Hindu* (4 and 5 October 1995). *The Hindu* from Madras, despite its name, still remains a widely circulated newspaper with a secular outlook.

8 Cf. J. Rosario Narchison, 'Theology in context: what and why?', *Theology for Our Times* (official organ of the ISET) 1 (June 1994), pp. 9–23 (p. 9).

9 Cf. J. Rosario Narchison, 'Mission in the context of religious fundamentalism: a few questions from Asia' in Joseph Mattam and Sebastian Kim (eds), *Dimensions of Mission in India* (Bombay: St Paul's, 1995), pp. 35–50 (p. 36).

10 In personal conversations with me M. A. Thomas used to refer to the instances in which he refused to accept foreign assistance simply because the funding agencies concerned laid down certain conditions on the 'ecumenical theology' he promoted.

11 M. A. Thomas, *Towards Wider Ecumenism* (Bangalore: Asian Trading Corporation, 1993), p. 111.

12 Quoted in Marcus Braybrooke, 'Discovering our oneness as servants of

God' in Ch. Srinivasa Rao (ed.), *Interfaith Dialogue and World Community* (Madras: CLS, 1991), pp. 108–16 (p. 115).

13 P. Chenchiah, 'The Christian message in a non-Christian world: a review of Dr Kraemer's book' in Job et al., *Rethinking Christianity*, p. 2 of the appendix. Emphasis added to the extract in view of the political dimension of religious pluralism to be treated in the next section of this chapter.

14 Thomas, *Towards Wider Ecumenism*, p. 111.

15 Michael Kinnamon, *Truth and Community: Diversity and Its Limits in the Ecumenical Movement* (Geneva: WCC, 1988), p. 100.

16 Paulo Freire, *Cultural Action for Freedom* (Baltimore: Penguin Books Inc., 1972), pp. 36–43.

17 ISET course outline as it is being sent out in advance to prospective participants.

18 Cf. S. Kappen, 'A new approach to theological education' in M. Amaladoss et al. (eds), *Theologizing in India* (Bangalore: Theological Publications in India, 1981), pp. 57–69 (pp. 57–8). See also Narchison, 'Theology in context', p. 16.

19 Thomas Berry, 'The earth a new context for religious unity' in Anne Lonergan and Caroline Richards (eds), *Thomas Berry and the New Cosmology* (Mystic, CT: Twenty-Third Publications, 1990), pp. 27–39 (p. 31).

20 View expressed during his informal interaction with the participants of one of the ISET courses in 1992. He passed away on 25 June 1993.

21 Cf. P. D. Devanandan, 'Contemporary Hindu secularism', *Religion and Society* 9 (1962), pp. 21–32.

22 The term 'religion' would be a very inadequate translation of the Sanskrit *dharma*.

23 As reported in *People's Reporter* (Bangalore bimonthly) from Bangalore (1–15 October 1995).

24 As frankly confessed by Samuel Amirtham in Mathai Zachariah (ed.), *Ecumenism in India: Essays in Honour of Rev. M. A. Thomas* (Delhi: ISPCK, 1980), p. 86.

25 K. C. Abraham, 'Pluralism as OIKOUMENE of solidarity' in K. C. Abraham (ed.), *New Horizons in Ecumenism: Essays in Honour of Bishop Samuel Amirthan* (Bangalore: BTESSC and BTTBPSA, 1993), pp. 118–40 (p. 119). See also M. M. Thomas, 'The church's mission in our pluralistic context', *Theology for Our Times* 2 (1995), pp. 5–11.

26 Note 13 above.

27 Quoted in P. D. Devanandan, 'Editorial', *Religion and Society* 9 (1962), p. 3; see also Rudolf C. Heredia, 'Secularism and secularization: nation building in a multi-religious society', *Towards Secular India* 1 (1995), pp. 44–63.

28 T. K. Oommen, 'On the varieties of communalism in India' in S. Arokiasamy (ed.), *Responding to Communalism: The Task of Religions and Theology* (Anand: Gujarat Sahitya Prakash, 1991), pp. 3–13 (p. 4).

29 Joseph Pathrapankal, 'The Bible and the context of religious pluralism', *Theology for Our Times* 1 (1994), pp. 39–52.

30 Paul F. Knitter, 'Cosmic confidence or preferential option?', *Bangalore Theological Forum* 23 (1991), pp. 1–29.

31 Tom F. Driver, 'The case for pluralism' in John Hick and Paul F. Knitter (eds), *The Myth of Christian Uniqueness* (London: SCM, 1988), pp. 203–18.

32 Driver, ibid., p. 205.

33 K. K. Katyal, 'Our dreams have become nightmares', *The Hindu* (13 August 1995); K. N. Panikkar, 'Ungodly men, unholy activities', *The Hindu* (22 October 1995).

5

Responsibilities for the future: toward an interfaith ethic

Paul F. Knitter

There are many people, especially within the halls of academia, who would have grave reservations about what I should like to propose in this chapter. I want to explore possibilities of an 'interfaith ethic'. I am suggesting that 'responsibility for the future' might provide the common ground on which religions can meet and fashion what Hans Küng and the World Parliament of Religions in Chicago in 1993 called a 'Global Ethic'. The hope is to form some kind of ethical unity out of the vast diversity of religious perspectives.

But such aspirations, for many of our contemporaries who bear or are burdened with a postmodern consciousness, are a very difficult, dangerous, perhaps even impossible, task. These critics, friendly and not-so-friendly, would warn of the pitfalls lurking within all universalizing programmes that try to set up any kind of 'common ground' between differing cultures or religions. There is no common ground that can sustain the vast variety of incommensurable particulars. Any attempt to formulate a common ground or a global ethic – especially when such attempts are organized by people who have most of the world's wealth and weapons – will end up smudging, or suffocating, or exploiting particularity. Thus, many would see the intent of this chapter, and much of what is going on in meetings like the World Parliament of Religions, as another camouflaged manoeuvre to control the interreligious and intercultural discourse with a Christian or Western agenda.

In what follows, I should like to respond to this postmodern criticism – not because I enjoy the bickerings of academics, but because I want what I am suggesting to be taken seriously. I shall offer some reasons why I think it is not only possible but also promising for members of all religious communities to take on responsibility for the future and to work toward what we can call an interfaith ethic. In more philosophical terms, I shall try to lay out what seem to me to be the 'conditions for the possibility' of an interfaith ethic. And I shall do this by drawing on data from both the religious and secular world which, I think and hope, many, if not most, representatives from differing religious traditions can agree on.

In the first part of this chapter, I shall try to show that the very nature of religion and religious experience, as we view it in its many-splendoured forms, indicates that all (or at least 'most') religious traditions have the capability, if not the established record, of affirming global responsibility as a common ground for interreligious encounters. As I shall argue in part 2, this capability is all the more enhanced today when our earth, in both its sufferings and its newly discovered mysteries, is becoming a locus for shared religious experience and vision. In part 3, I shall take up the sticky question of how an interfaith ethic might adjudicate between competing ethical claims – that is, how eco-human 'justice' or 'well-being' can serve as a universal criterion for truth without becoming a new foundational or absolute norm for truth.

1 Global responsibility – can all religions endorse it?

Both from what we can see in the world of religions and from what the academicians tell us, religion, in all its exuberant forms, has to do with changing this world for the better. Yes, religion has to do with what is called God or the Ultimate, and with life after death, and with altering or expanding our consciousness – but it also has to do with confronting, specifying and then repairing what is wrong in the way human beings live their lives together in this world. Whether you call it evil or ignorance or incompleteness, there's something wrong with the state of the world as it is, and religion wants to do something about it.

In other words, the religions call on what is more than human (at least the human as we now experience it) in order to transform or liberate the human. In the words of V. Harvey, '[W]hen we call something religious we ordinarily mean a perspective expressing a dominating interest in certain universal and elemental features of human existence as those features *bear on the human desire for liberation and authentic existence*'.[1] To transform the human context will mean, generally, to oppose or resist the forces that stand in the way of change or newness. Thus, David Tracy, ever cautious about general statements regarding religions, can recognize:

> Above all, the religions are exercises in resistance. Whether seen as Utopian visions or believed in as revelations of Ultimate Reality, the religions reveal various possibilities for human freedom ... When not domesticated as sacred canopies for the status quo nor wasted by their

own self-contradictory grasps at power, the religions live by resisting. The chief resistance of religions is to more of the same.[2]

The mystical–prophetic dipolarity of all religion

Naturally, in claiming that all religions are world-oriented and bear an energy that can change the earth, I am not saying that this is all they contain or that this is their only concern. Besides this world-transforming energy, there is another category of power that is just as important. Scholars have spoken of both the *prophetic* and the *mystical* power of religion.

In each religious tradition we can find both mystical and prophetic experiences and visions. And the line between them is not so much a wall that separates but a bond that unites and mutually nourishes. So we must admit and encourage the *mystical–prophetic dipolarity* that vibrates and flows back and forth within all religious traditions. This dipolar energy of religion animates a twofold project, each aspect essential, each calling to and dependent on the other, to transform both the within and the without, to alter inner consciousness and social consciousness, to bring about peace of the heart and peace in the world, stirring the individual to an earnest spiritual praxis and also to a bold political praxis.

The dynamic and call of this mystical–prophetic dipolarity is what tells Christians that they can love God only when they are loving their neighbour, or Buddhists that wisdom is not possible without compassion, or Hindus that the yoga of knowledge or devotion must be combined with the yogas of action in this world. Neither the mystical nor the prophetic is more fundamental, more important; each calls to, and has its existence in, the other.

Certainly the dipolarity, or the balance, will be maintained differently within different religions, or within different denominations of the same religion, or at different stages within an individual's personal journey. Frequently – all too frequently – the balance is not maintained; and then we have mystics whose spirituality becomes self-indulgent, insensitive, or irresponsible; or we have prophets whose actions become self-serving, intolerant, or violent. When the mutual feed-back system between the mystical and the prophetic within a religion breaks down, the religion becomes either an opium to avoid the world or an indult to exploit it.

So today, 'In all the major religious traditions, there is a search for new ways to unite those mystical and prophetic trajectories . . . '.[3] In an age in which we are horrifyingly aware of human and ecological sufferings, and of the devastating dangers seeded within this suffering, every religion is being challenged to rediscover the prophetic power of its tradition and to unite it to the mystical. The prophetic power is there, perhaps beneath a mystical overgrowth, perhaps hidden in narratives and symbols which spoke to a different age and which are in need of revising for this age. If this power is not tapped or refurbished, the religious tradition will lose its ability to speak to and engage the many persons today who feel the prophetic challenge of our suffering world.

A shared diagnosis and remedy for the human predicament

But I think we can go a step further. As we survey the vast terrain of religious history and experience, we can identify, I suggest, not only an undercurrent of concern for transforming this world, not only a dipolar flow between mystical and prophetic experience, but also an analogously similar *diagnosis* of what is wrong with our world and a *prescription* for what must be done to fix it. The operative word in that last sentence is 'analogously'. I am not suggesting that all the religions of the world are really proposing identical or essentially similar soteriologies – programmes for how the world and we humans are to be 'saved'. Rather, my experience in interreligious dialogue and social action has been that when one plunges into the vast diversity of religious analyses of what's wrong with the human predicament and how it might be set aright, when one wrestles with the very real and powerful *differences* in these analyses and programmes, one finds that the differences one is wrestling with turn out, for the most part, to be friends rather than foes.

More specifically, it seems that the analogous similarities between the differing religious views of humanity's fundamental problems take shape around the issues of the *nature of the self* and how the self can be understood or experienced differently. According to the myths, doctrines and ethical admonitions of most religions, humankind's woes flow from a pool of disunity and dis-ease fed by a false notion of the self. The problem, in other words, has to do with the way we understand and live out our sense of who we are. Either we understand ourselves incorrectly or our selves, in their present state, are corrupted or incomplete. In either case, something has to happen to the self, either notionally or in reality. We either have to understand or experience our selves differently, or our selves have to be infused with new or healing energies. Whether the fix is cognitional from within or ontological from without, it has to lead to a different way of acting in and of relating to the world around us.

So the problem recognized analogously by different religions has to do with separation or selfishness: and the remedy has to do with relationship and mutuality. In many different ways, most (all?) religions seek to convert the energies of one's self from a centripetal to a centrifugal movement and so to broaden the focus of concern from not only me or us (egocentricity) to Other or others (altruism). We have to find ourselves outside of ourselves; to realize who we are, we have to experience ourselves as part of something that is greater than what we understand ourselves to be right now. John Hick, using Western terminology, seeks to summarize all this by describing the analogously common goal of most religions as a shift from self-centredness to Reality-centredness.[4]

Admittedly, as feminist critics point out, such ideals of a selfless self have been fashioned by patriarchal religions – that means, by men whose primary 'sin' has been an inflated self that abuses other selves, and not by women whose primary sin has been a deflated self that allows itself to be abused by others. Thus, what I am proposing here as a diagnosis common to all religions requires a feminist hermeneutics of suspicion that will assure that the selfless self does not become the enslaved or subordinated self.[5] Still, I think feminists would agree that the 'saved self' or new self is one that is sustained in the web of mutuality rather than in the cell of egocentricity.[6]

2 *The earth: common ground for encountering the sacred*

So far, our proposal has been that differing religions can and must share a global responsibility for eco-human wellbeing and justice. Even though many contemporary scholars are extremely uneasy with such a universal proposal (and would want to cut it up into socially-constructed pieces), I think that global responsibility for the future enables religious persons to take an even bolder step. So I would like to explain why I, along with others, am convinced that the kind of global responsibility we have been talking about can be not only a shared commitment but also a *shared context for religious experience*, feeding and reforming our different religious traditions. Global responsibility is not only an *ethical task* that all religious persons can take up together but also a *religious task* and a source of shared experiences by which believers from different communities can better understand and communicate each other's religious stories and language.

To feel global responsibility, to give oneself to the task of struggling for *soteria* in this tormented world, to join hands with victims and to experience victimization in the struggle for justice, to feel claimed by the sacredness of the earth and called to protect the earth – such human experiences and activities constitute a universally available locus, an arena open to all, where persons of different religious backgrounds can feel the presence and empowerment of that for which religious language seems appropriate.

Working for eco-human justice becomes a common context in which we find ourselves using our different religious stories and symbols. So our experiences of injustice are different, as is our language; but at the same time, these differing words are flowing from a common experiential process. There is, I dare say, something 'common' within the diversity. We are 'communing' with that which sustains or might be the goal of our various traditions. Working together for justice becomes, or can become, a *communicatio in sacris* – a communication in the Sacred – available to us beyond our churches and temples. But just how does this work?

Extra mundum nulla salus – *Outside the world there is no salvation*

Edward Schillebeeckx helps us to understand how global responsibility can be a 'communication in the Sacred' when he takes the long-standing ecclesiocentric dictum *extra ecclesiam nulla salus* (outside the church there is no salvation) and turns it on its head to read *extra mundum nulla salus* (outside the world there is no salvation). Here Schillebeeckx is speaking not just to his fellow Christians but is announcing a reality that he feels can be recognized and affirmed by all religious persons. It is precisely in the confrontation and struggle with a world littered with limitations and inadequacies (to put it philosophically), or with suffering and injustice (to put it existentially), that we can, and do, encounter the divine. Again, his language is Christian, but the experience he is describing can, I believe, be caught and illuminated by a variety of religious symbols and narratives.

Schillebeeckx describes a basically identical worldly process in which many people, from a variety of religions and cultures, find themselves today. They encounter situations of 'negative experience of contrast' before which they find themselves pronouncing, first, a spontaneous and forceful 'no' to what the situation is, and then a resolute 'yes' to how it might be transformed. In this explosive 'no' and then in this determined 'yes', we find the first stirrings of religious experience – what Schillebeeckx calls 'pre-religious experiences'. This 'natural' or 'given' human response of resistance leading to hope and action is the raw material, as it were, out of which religious experience or faith can take form. This is what Schillebeeckx means by 'no salvation outside the world'; it is in the confrontation with and struggle to improve the world that the reality of the Transcendent/Immanent makes itself felt. For Schillebeeckx, the praxis of involvement in the world has a primacy in

Responsibilities for the future: toward an interfaith ethic   81

religious experience and in what Christians call revelation.[7]

My suggestion, therefore, is that just as persons from various spir- itualities have sought for a multifaith *communicatio in sacris* – a sharing of religious experience – in ashrams and monasteries, and in participa- tion in each other's meditational or prayer practices, so today they can also share their religious experiences and language in the concrete praxis of a global spirituality and the struggle for eco-human justice that such responsibility demands. We can commune in the sacred as we commune in the sufferings of our world. Thus, a group of sixteen representatives of various religious paths in India could conclude their dialogue with this joint statement:

> When we stand for justice and freedom and for people's right to life
> with dignity, we stand for those realities and values, in terms of which
> *all faiths image the Mystery of the Divine* ... The downtrodden people
> with their history of hope and struggle is the *locus*, the place, of
> authentic encounter with God. In confronting injustice and working for
> a new India, a new world, where people are equal and free, and where
> resources are for all, there exists a profound spirituality even if it is not
> recognised, made explicit.[8]

The threatened earth: a common ethical challenge

But there is another way – broader and both more challenging and promising – in which our world can provide common ground for dialogue toward an interfaith ethic. I am not talking here about what some are proposing as a 'common creation story', based on what science tells us about the origins and functioning of the universe; they suggest that this creation or cosmological story can serve as the umbrella myth, as it were, under which all the creation stories of the world can be reordered and assembled together alongside each other.[9] For many, however, such a common cosmological story is highly suspect, not because it is proposed as *common* but because it is proposed by Western *science*. Rather than find myself caught in the tangle of such justified concerns, I prefer to point out, in what we know about the earth today, not so much a common creation story but, rather, a common *ethical story*.

I am suggesting that our present-day 'common knowledge' about the earth can provide religions not only with common knowledge about our shared origins in the big bang and the wondrous complexity of evolution but also, and more clearly and urgently, with common knowledge about a shared ethical task and shared guidelines to carry out that task. It is especially on the ethical level that the so-called 'universe story' can exercise a practical unifying force among the religions.

The chapter in the universe story that is presently being lived out and written might fittingly be titled, in the words of biologist Edward O. Wilson: 'Is humanity suicidal?'[10] We are indeed 'flirting with the extinction of our species' as we witness and cause the extinction of thousands of other species, and in general strangle the life-sustaining capacities of the planet. The task of preventing this suicide, and the broader geocide, is the most compelling and unsettling ethical imperative facing humankind today. 'In spite of continuing political tensions among nations, the most dangerous threat to the world's well-being is not war but the closing down of the earth's most basic systems, which support us and all other forms of life.'[11] Not to respond to this threat and this ethical imperative is to renounce or diminish one's humanity. Because this is true for peoples in all cultures, of all religions (in different degrees, of course, for the impoverished campesino than for the multi-national executive), our common universe story, with its ecological awareness and demands, provides us with the motivation and the means to break the roadblock that many people try to place before any kind of a common ethical venture based on common ethical criteria.

To the postmodern insistence that every value or every moral project is but an individual social construction valid only for its own backyard, to the refusal of many today to endorse any kind of universal or 'meta' discourse that would rally the troops in a united campaign, we can hold up our common universe story that tells us we are all interrelated in our origins, in our functioning *and* in our responsibility for saving our species and endangered planet. With Charlene Spretnak, I think we can speak of 'the "metadiscourse" of the universe' which can link our individual discourses, or of the 'grand cosmologic' that can inform the logic of all cultures. Before we are located in our separate, diverse cultural–religious houses, we are located, more deeply and decisively and responsibly, in the cosmic neighbourhood, in the one world in which we all share and which connects us all with each other and which, today, pleads with us for its own salvation.[12]

There is, therefore, a 'place' where we all stand together, where we share both common experiences, concerns and responsibilities: our earth – beautiful in its mysterious connectedness and evolution but also menaced in the devastation that the human species has wrought upon it. This earth provides the religions not only with a religious community in which they possibly can share myths of origin, but also, and more imperatively, with an ethical community in which they can and must identify and defend common criteria of truth. In their basic content, such criteria will probably be something like those being worked out by international ecological groups, especially non-governmental – criteria that seek to balance the promotion of life for individuals and for eco-systems. I am not claiming that such universal ethical criteria are ready made or that they can be neatly articulated in a kind of ecological decalogue. But I am stating that the universe story, which today we read as a drama whose outcome is still to be told, can provide religions with the materials and perspectives with which successfully, though never finally, to work out global ecological norms.[13]

So when our efforts toward an interfaith ethic based on justice are challenged with the fitting question of 'Whose justice are you talking about?', we can give one clear and equally challenging response: the earth's justice! Yes, the critics are right – every understanding of justice is socially mediated and motivated. But here is one form of justice that we must all not only be concerned about but also in some way agree on: all nations and religions must devote themselves to the common task of saving and sustaining the integrity and life-giving powers of the planet. If the job isn't done jointly, it won't really be done! It's as simple, and yet as profound, as that. So the hope expressed by Thomas Berry is as idealistic as it is imperative, and it seems to me that we have no choice but to endorse it: 'Concern for the well-being of the planet is the one concern that hopefully will bring the nations [and the religions] of the world into an inter-nation [and inter-religious] community.'[14]

3 Eco-human well-being: a universal criterion for truth

Having proposed in part 1 that all religions show the capability of genuine concern for human wellbeing in this world, having described in part 2 how the state of the present world (especially the drama of the universe story) is calling forth this capability, I must recognize the stubborn truth that there is no clear, identifiable unity among the religious communities on how we are to respond to the needs of this suffering planet, no agreement, yet, on the essential elements in an interfaith ethic. The spectre of diversity once again rears its defiant head and announces the counter-claim: 'Okay, the sufferings of people and planet may present the religions with a common problem. But just because you have a common problem (maybe even a common dia-gnosis of the problem), you don't have the assurance of a common answer.' Thus, the question of 'Whose justice?' can never be simply or totally dismissed. The diversity of religious experience and traditions will not allow it.

David Tracy states the problem more academically and more point-edly:

There are family resemblances among the religions. But as far as I can

see, there is no single essence, no one content of enlightenment or
revelation, no one way of emancipation or liberation to be found in all
that plurality ... there are different interpretations of what way we
should follow to move from a fatal self-centeredness to a liberating
Reality-centeredness ... The responses of the religions, their various
narratives, doctrines, symbols, and their often conflicting accounts of
the way to authentic liberation are at least as different as they are
similar. They are clearly not the same.[15]

Eco-human justice: a cross-cultural criterion

How can we fashion consensus out of such stubborn diversity? How
can we mediate between two differing views about what will ensure
authentic liberation? In a particular context, for instance, a Buddhist
may call for the total selflessness of non-violence, while a Christian may
urge the self-giving of armed resistance. How might a shared commitment to global responsibility and eco-human justice help adjudicate the
truth between them?

David Tracy tries to answer that question. He outlines three general
criteria for religious truth which he thinks could be acceptable to
persons of different religious traditions and which therefore can enable
them to reach joint judgements:

a   'The truth of a religion is, like the truth of its nearest cousin, art,
     primordially the truth of manifestation.'[16] In religion, we know
     something to be so because it *manifests* or reveals itself to us; we
     know it because, like the beauty of art, we feel it. More practically,
     it *makes a claim* on us; it grasps or lays hold of us. So, if the stories or
     rituals of your religion can tug at and claim my heart, if I feel their
     truth manifested before me at least as a 'suggestive possibility',[17] I
     can share your truth, and so we can come to mutual agreement.
b   But what touches the heart must also listen to the head. Even
     though there is no cross-cultural consensus on what 'reasonability'
     means or requires, Tracy believes that all religions will recognize
     the need for some kind of 'cognitive criteria of coherence with what
     we otherwise know or, more likely, believe to be the case'.[18]
c   Finally, there must also be 'ethical-political criteria on the personal
     and social consequences of our beliefs'.[19] How do our religious
     experience and beliefs make for a better world, both our own and
     that of society?

Tracy's first two criteria – revelatory power and rational coherence –
are much more subjectively or culturally conditioned than his third
criterion – the ethical demands arising from starvation or destruction of

the rain forests (though all ethical responses are to some extent cultur-ally coloured). Ethical and liberative criteria, insofar as they are directed toward problems or issues that are truly common to us all, are better able to serve as the starting point or foundation with which we can move on to discuss the revelatory power and the rational coherence of our individual truth claims.

So of the three cross-cultural criteria for working toward shared assessments of truth among the incorrigible diversity of world religions – personal experience, cognitive coherence and ethical fruits – it is the last criterion, it seems to me, that is 'most cross-cultural'. Questions concerning the ethical fruits of a particular belief or practice – that is, whether it does remove suffering and promote wellbeing – provide common ground on which persons of differing traditions can stand and effectively discuss their differences and work toward consensus. The critical data regarding the ethical effects of one's claims are, as it were, much more 'at hand' than are appeals to one's religious experience or to what makes rational sense.

If followers of various religious traditions can agree in the beginning that whatever else their experience of truth or of the divine or of enlightenment may bring about, it must always promote greater eco-human wellbeing and remove the sufferings of our world, then they have a shared reference point from which to affirm or criticize each other's claims. Such ethical concerns do not provide immediate solu-tions to interreligious disagreements; but they do constitute a walkable path toward such solutions.

So I would agree with Francis Schüssler Fiorenza when he proposes 'solidarity with the suffering' as the source of criteria that will enable persons from diverse cultures and religions to come to shared conclu-sions about truth and value and action.[20] Precisely because human and ecological suffering is both *universal* and *immediate* it can serve all religious persons as a common context and criteriological resource for assessing religious truth-claims. In its universality, human and eco-logical suffering confronts and affects us all; in its immediacy, it has a raw reality and challenge that is somehow beyond our differing inter-pretations of it. This is why 'suffering brings us to the bedrock of human existence and cuts through the hermeneutical circle'.[21] The stark image of a child starving because of poverty or of a lake polluted because of chemical dumping has an immediacy that breaks through our differing cultural interpretations of it. It stares us in the face and questions us before we fully understand or interpret it. It is this questioning face of the suffering that enables religions to face and question each other and come to joint assessments of truth. Thus, a concern for ethical-political criteria in the face of suffering can work cross-culturally.

But in order to work, it is not enough that the participants in interreligious dialogue simply 'bear in mind' the reality of the suffering of the victims of human or ecological injustice; it is not enough that they all announce to each other and the world that they are 'globally responsible' for the future. If ethical-political criteria resulting from 'solidarity with the suffering' are really to bear fruit in the elaboration of an interfaith ethic, the suffering victims must have a 'hermeneutical privilege' in dialogical decision-making about such an ethic; this means that the suffering oppressed themselves, together with those who can speak for the oppressed species and earth, will have to be not simply the *object* of the dialogue but active *participants* in it. If their voices are to be heard, they will have to be present as they have not generally been present within the arena of interreligious dialogue.

The suffering, the victims, will have to have an active part in determining the agenda for the dialogue – the procedure and format, yes, the place and the language, too! Just how all this can be arranged is not easy to say, for certainly this has not been the style or the practice of dialogical conferences as they have been planned and practised over the past decades; the excluded will now have to be included. If religious spokespersons are serious about basing their discussions on ethical-political criteria and on global responsibility, then they will have to prove this seriousness by inviting to the dialogue those most affected by present ethical and political realities.

But what is required is more than simply inviting the suffering and oppressed to the table of dialogue. If their voices are not only to be heard but also to be understood, if the reality of their suffering and ethical concerns is to be felt and not just registered, then somehow all the participants in the dialogue need to be *actively involved in the praxis* of working against eco-human injustice and promoting more life-giving, just ethical-political policies in the structures of governments and economics. One can hear the message of the suffering only if one is struggling, and therefore suffering, together with them. Dialogical conversation must include, in some way, dialogical praxis for liberation and wellbeing. Just what this means and how it can be carried out will vary from context to context.

With these other voices representing the suffering of humanity and of the earth actively present in our interreligious discourse, participants will be able to apply ethical-political criteria all the more realistically and effectively. Those representing the marginalized and oppressed can serve, as it were, as 'arbiters' or a 'court of appeal' when there are differing views among the religious spokespersons as to just what are the ethical fruits of a particular religious claim. Such decisions, in other words, are not to be made only, or primarily, by the 'religious experts'.

The persons directly affected will give witness about just how their lives have been changed and enhanced, or limited and threatened, by a particular religious conviction or behaviour. They will make known, for instance, how images of God as transcendent or immanent affect their attitudes to this world, how beliefs in karma or after-life have contributed to their wellbeing now, how non-violent or armed forms of resistance can improve their situation. Not that their views or experiences will be the final verdict in any discussion. Still, I am convinced that their voices will generally be an effective, if not decisive, help in the difficult task of honouring the diversity of religious views and yet formulating out of that diversity decisions and programmes that will promote global responsibility and an interfaith ethic.

We must hope that the individual religious communities of the world will build a 'community of communities', a paradoxical but actual community in which we belong both to our own religion and culture and yet genuinely participate in the global community struggling for eco-human justice and wellbeing. It will be a community in which we are both particularists and universalists, making strong claims on the basis of our particular religious convictions but knowing that such claims might be relativized in the wider conversation with other strong claims and with the even stronger demand to remove human and ecological suffering.

If there are those who say such an ethical community of communities among religions is a pipe dream, then I respond respectfully but firmly that we have no choice today but to dream such dreams.

Notes

1 Quoted in David Tracy, *Dialogue with the Other: The Inter-Religious Dialogue* (Grand Rapids: Eerdmans, 1990), p. 54. Emphasis mine.

2 David Tracy, *Plurality and Ambiguity: Hermeneutics, Religion, Hope* (New York: Harper & Row, 1987), p. 84. Therefore, according to Raimundo Panikkar, even to raise the question whether religion has anything to do with changing this world is to fall victim to a dualism that runs contrary to the ideals of most, if not all, religions. It is a dualism between God and the world, or religion and politics, that stems, not from the content of religious experience, but from external efforts (especially in the West) to spiritualize, or privatize religion and thus dilute its political power: see Raimundo Panikkar, 'Religion or politics: the western dilemma' in Peter H. Merkle and Ninian Smart (eds), *Religion and Politics in the Modern World* (New York: University Press, 1983), p. 52. Gandhi, then, was right when he announced 'I can say without the slightest hesitation and yet in all humility that those who say that religion has nothing to do with politics do not know what religion means': *My Autobiography* (Boston:

Beacon Press, 1957), p. 504. Or maybe they know very well what it means, but seek to deny or stifle the power of religion.

3 David Tracy, 'God, dialogue and solidarity: a theologian's refrain', *The Christian Century* (10 October 1990), p. 900.

4 John Hick, *An Interpretation of Religion* (New Haven, CT: Yale University Press, 1989), pp. 299–309.

5 Valerie Saiving, 'The human situation: a feminine view' in Carol Christ and Judith Plaskow (eds), *Womanspirit Rising: A Feminist Reader in Religion* (San Francisco: Harper & Row, 1979), pp. 25–42; Judith Plaskow, *Sex, Sin, and Grace: Women's Experience and the Theologies of Reinhold Niebuhr and Paul Tillich* (Lanham, MD: University Press of America, 1980), pp. 51–94.

6 Catherine Keller, *From a Broken Web: Separation, Sexism, and Self* (Boston: Beacon Press, 1986).

7 Edward Schillebeeckx, *The Church: The Human Story of God* (New York: Crossroad, 1990), pp. 5–15.

8 Final report of the consultation organized by the Indian regional committee of EATWOT (Ecumenical Association of Third World Theologians), 27 February–2 March 1989 in Madras. Privately distributed.

9 Thomas Berry and Brian Swimme, *The Universe Story* (HarperSanFrancisco, 1992); Sallie McFague, 'Cosmology and Christianity: implications of the common creation story for theology' in Sheila Greeve Devaney (ed.), *Theology at the End of Modernity* (Philadelphia: Trinity Press International, 1991), pp. 19–40.

10 Edward O. Wilson, 'Is humanity suicidal?', *New York Times Magazine* (30 May 1992), pp. 24–9.

11 McFague, 'Cosmology and Christianity', p. 20.

12 Charlene Spretnak, *States of Grace: The Recovery of Meaning in the Postmodern Age* (HarperSanFrancisco, 1991), pp. 81, 105.

13 One set of such general norms was suggested by the International Coordinating Committee on Religion and the Earth for the Rio Conference. The committee formulated a statement of 'Ethics for living' which called on all people to live: sustainably (with a concern for the present *and* for the future), justly, frugally, peacefully, interdependently, knowledgeably (recognizing the need for ecological education) and holistically (fostering the whole person, spiritually, physically, intellectually). See 'An earth charter', distributed by the International Coordinating Committee on Religion and the Earth, Wainwright House, 260 Stuyvesant Avenue, New York, NY 10580.

14 Thomas Berry, *The Dream of the Earth* (San Francisco: Sierra Club Books, 1988), p. 218.

15 Tracy, *Plurality and Ambiguity*, pp. 90, 92.

16 Tracy, *Dialogue with the Other*, p. 43.

17 Ibid., p. 40.

18 Tracy, 'God, dialogue, and solidarity', p. 901.

19 Ibid.

20 Francis Schüssler Fiorenza, 'Theological and religious studies: the contest of the faculties' in Barbara G. Wheeler and Edward Farley (eds), *Shifting Boundaries: Contextual Approaches to the Structure of Theological Education* (Louisville: Westminster/John Knox, 1991), pp. 133–4.
21 Ibid., p. 135.

6

The religions and the birth of a new humanity

Pia Gyger

The theme of my address today is 'the religions and the birth of a new humanity'. In speaking to you, I first want to say a few words about the epoch in which we live. First of all, I should like to interpret from an evolutionary standpoint all that we see and hear every day in the mass media. Secondly, I should like to share some thoughts with you about the possibilities and chances for a common commitment by the world religions to overcome the crises of our times. Thirdly, I wish to show, by means of a few concrete examples, how the institution in which I work attempts to make a contribution to more peace and unity in the world.

1 Understanding our times from an evolutionary perspective

As we all know, we live in a time in which the further existence of humanity and the planet earth is threatened. A small percentage of the world's population lives in comfort and luxury while about 950 million people live in crushing poverty. Every day about 40,000 children die of hunger and about 30 million people die every year of malnutrition. In spite of this inhuman situation, the countries of the world continue to provide about 1.8 million US dollars every minute for military armaments. These are the millions that we so urgently require for the rehabilitation of our planet. Preventing war, achieving global disarmament and creating a new world peace order ... these are among the most important tasks of any nation.

However, it is not humanity alone which suffers. The entire planet is suffering. Every day an animal or plant species becomes extinct. Dying trees, rivers and oceans are the result of air and water pollution.[1] The ecological problems that beset us cannot be solved by any single country. In order to come to meaningful solutions to these worsening problems, humanity crucially requires new, transnational political

90

structures. The national policies of individual countries must be brought step-by-step into agreement with the planetary needs of humanity and the earth. Humanity must, if it wishes to survive, achieve on the political level what it has already achieved for the most part on the technical and economic level: a global network which connects everyone with everyone else.

The process toward greater political unity in Europe and everywhere else in the world is a necessary evolutionary development which cannot be avoided. Our planet and humanity have developed in all phases of their history according to the same principle: becoming part of something greater through unification.

- – Elementary particles attract each other.
- – Atoms combine with each other.
- – Cells become cell tissue.
- – People become humanity.

The readiness for new synthesis and integration is the driving force of all evolution.

People become humanity. This is the evolutionary step in which we find ourselves today. The birth of humanity toward a unified organism is occurring in us and through us. And, as is the case with every birth, the process is painful and accompanied by crises. Speaking in the language of evolution we can say: The transition to a new and higher synthesis and integration is always characterized by the disintegration of the constituent and stabilizing factors of the old form.[2] It is this which creates the exigency of our present times. The old values are no longer sustaining, the old structures are suffocating. This creates chaos and uncertainty and has the effect that many individuals and groups cling to traditional ways and isolate themselves from any new opening or integration. And yet, if we wish to survive as a species, the only way is to understand ourselves first as world citizens, and then as Swiss, Americans or Dutch. We must realize (and begin to act according to the realization) that the welfare of the individual and the welfare of a nation can only be guaranteed if they agree with the needs of the total organism of humanity. Only when we realize and act in this way will we have a chance for survival. Expressing this in political terms, we can say that, today and in the future, we must work together to create a pan-federal, democratic world community in which individuals and groups learn to live in synergy with the needs of the total organism of humanity. As long as we remain incapable of imagining how we can awake to the consciousness of unity of everything with everything else, as long as we are incapable of giving form in our life and actions to this implicit unity of all things, we prevent unity and peace on our planet through our dualistic thinking. It is vitally important that we have the courage to allow the vision of a more reasonable and peacefully unified humanity to take form in us. As a psychologist, I am aware of the necessity of recognizing and understanding negative and destructive elements. But this is only the first step toward healing. If we only remain on the level of seeing our problems, we reinforce negative energies by being fixed on the destructive aspect. We also strengthen the destructive element when we use our energies primarily to combat those destructive elements. 'Not fighting against the lack, but being there for what is lacking.' This educational rule is also true regarding the global problems of humanity. We not only have the ability to bring about our own destruction. We also have the equal ability to transform our destructive elements of consciousness if we are prepared to allow ourselves to be gifted with the healing and guiding visions. That brings me to the second part of my address.

2 Possibilities and chances of common commitment of the world religions toward more peace in the world

The principle of plurality is an evolutionary reality. Whether it be the variety of species in plant and animal kingdom, or the variety of races in humanity, the principle of plurality is at work. Plurality, in its essence, contains both a great treasure as well as a great tribulation. The treasure is found in the tremendous possibility of completion if we accept the plurality of races, peoples and religions in the world. The tribulation of plurality is the task of overcoming our fear of the strange and different.[3]

'Unification is commensurate to suffering.' That is how Teilhard de Chardin described the process of 'planetization' or unification of the family of humanity. In order to experience the treasure hidden in plurality we must first accept the tribulation that plurality brings. We must learn to rid ourselves of our fears in coming into contact with that which is foreign to us. We must learn consciously to seek and nurture contacts with people of other races, cultures and religions. To the extent that we are capable of that, we will experience the treasure of plurality. We will experience that the encounter with the foreign enriches and renews us as well. This is also true regarding encounters among the world religions.

We have come here to share with each other about the plurality of the religions. Those who spoke before me have examined the chances and dangers of plurality from different standpoints. I don't need to repeat what they have said. My task is to motivate all of us here today to recognize plurality among the different religions as a potential for world peace and help create a situation in which that potential becomes active in us and through us.

Humanity desperately requires that the world religions work toward a world ethos which will show all of us the basic values which must be realized in order that we can bear up under the birth of the organism mankind.

I am extremely grateful to Hans Küng and all those representatives of different religions who created and adopted basic elements for a world ethos at the second Parliament of the World Religions in 1993.

The four directives proclaimed by the parliament as a world ethos toward which all world religions should strive are crucial for the survival of humankind.

Imagine the possibilities if all the religions would devote their energies toward nurturing a culture of non-violence and reverence for life, a culture of solidarity and a just economic order, a culture of tolerance and a life in truthfulness, a culture of equal rights and partnership for men and women![4]

As I was preparing this address, I heard the news that the Vienna Conference had failed to achieve a ban on land-mines and anti-personnel mines. A million personnel mines are produced every year. In the last ten years more than a million people, including many children, have been killed by mines. Hundreds of millions of land-mines have already been planted, ready to kill at any time. Large stretches of arable land have become unusable as a result. And this in countries where there is great hunger, such as in Afghanistan. You can buy a mine for four dollars. Defusing a mine costs 300 to 1,000 dollars. At the present rate of defusing it will take 4,300 years to rid our contaminated land of mines! Although UN Secretary General Boutros-Ghali pleaded passionately for a ban on land and anti-personnel mines, the conference in Vienna failed to reach that goal. Take a few moments to let those facts sink in. In the last ten years, a million people have been killed by mines. Millions of mines are contaminating our planet. It will require thousands of years just to repair the damage that has already been done. And in spite of this, the world community is neither ready nor willing to pass a ban on mines! How will coming generations deal with the problems that we bequeath them on this planet? The sufferings of humankind and the sufferings of our planet demand a commitment of all religions to reverence for life, worldwide justice and solidarity, tolerance and worldwide partnership between men and women. Dialogue among religions is not a matter of comparing the various experiences of an ultimate reality and discovering which experiences are deeper or more authentic. It is a question of the survival of humanity and the planet earth! It means that leaders of all religions show their members that no people has any more right to this planet than another, and that we only have a chance for survival if we can experience ourselves as a family of humanity and learn to act in that way. The world's politicians cannot alone bring about the changes that the world so desperately needs. These people require the guidance and support of religious leaders. Humanity needs a world ethos, recognized by all religions in order to allow unity and peace to bear fruit in the world. We all have the opportunity to put our energies to work in realizing those goals. And with this I come to the final section of my address.

3 The Lassalle-Haus, an experimental laboratory taking steps in the direction of interreligious dialogue and a world ethos

The Lassalle-Haus in Switzerland is a centre for spirituality and social consciousness. In November 1995, it opened an Institute for Spirituality in Economics and Politics. The programme of the new institution is characterized by the insight that there can be no peace in the world without peace among the religions.

The institute has the following tasks:

1 Holding regular international symposia and meetings in the area of interreligious dialogue
2 Working out guidelines for interreligious and interspiritual dialogue and putting them into practice
3 Developing aspects of an interreligious dialogue culture
4 Making people aware of the necessity of a world ethos and promoting its realization
5 Developing realistic visions on how a democratic-federalist world community can be created
6 Developing and testing models for constructive conflict-solving for management in economics and politics, and propagating those models in seminars.[5]

These programme points show that the institute does not just want to offer meetings for transformation of consciousness. The goal of the institute is a common commitment of Buddhists and Christians in the birth of humanity toward a unified organism. This common commitment is only possible if a culture of dialogue is created beforehand by Buddhists and Christians. It is only possible if they have worked together towards a common denominator upon which they can build their project work. In the past two years, the working group of Buddhists and Christians advising the Lassalle-Haus has worked together with the Zen Community of New York to create those foundations. What is the common denominator upon which Buddhists and

Christians wish to build their work in the Lassalle-Haus? It is the insight that anything truly new does not grow through the dissolution of differences and opposites, but only through the unification of opposites. Thus, in creating a culture of dialogue, we are not attempting to level out differences between Christianity and Buddhism. On the contrary! It is regressive to immerse ourselves in differences and eliminate differences that have developed in terms of contents and institutions. It is not a levelling out of differences among different religious traditions that will achieve the new wholeness that is so necessary. What we need now is an existential encounter among different traditions and the mutual transformation that occurs as a result. This insight is the foundation for the common project work of Buddhists and Christians at Lassalle-Haus. Together we attempt to find ways whereby differences in our views of the world and humanity are not a hindrance to our common commitment, but fruitful in the task of achieving more unity in the world. Let me cite a few concrete examples.

In May 1996, Tetsugen Glassman, director of the Zen Community of New York, Father Niklaus Brantschen, Director of the Lassalle-Haus, and I held a second street sesshin in the middle of the Zürich drug scene. Immediately following that sesshin there was a meeting in Lassalle-Haus with the theme of 'Buddhists and Christians for a more peaceful world'. Our main goal was to seek concrete possibilities for a common commitment toward peace.

In December 1996, a 'Peace Sesshin' was held in Lassalle-Haus under the direction of Glassman Roshi, Fr Brantschen and myself. That sesshin included ordination of Buddhist and Christian peacemakers. At the same time, the Lassalle-Haus is working together with the Zen Community of New York on a curriculum which should make it easier to find both inner and outer ways for all those who want to become involved actively in the quest for more peace, justice, a world ethos and preservation of the earth.[6]

With these concrete examples I would like to end my address. It was my wish to motivate those gathered here today to engage their talents so that the treasure of plurality can become fruitful at the birth of a new humanity.

Notes

1 Taken from data from various UN commissions.

2 See Pierre Teilhard de Chardin, *The Phenomenon of Man* (London: Collins, 1959); *Man's Place in Nature* (London: Collins, 1966); *The Future of Man* (London: Collins, 1965).

3 See Teilhard de Chardin, *Human Energy* (London: Collins, 1969).

4 Hans Küng and Karl-Josef Kuschel (eds), *A Global Ethic: The Declaration of the Parliament of the World's Religions* (London: SCM, 1993).
5 Refer to: Institute for Spirituality in Politics and the Economy, Lassalle-Haus, CH-6313 Edlibach/Zug, Switzerland.
6 In May 1997 there was an interreligious conference in Lassalle-Haus with the theme of 'Spirituality and the environment: the contribution of Buddhists and Christians to preservation of the earth'.

Index